I Used To Be Normal

How I discovered that there's more to life than I
ever imagined

I Used To Be Normal

How I discovered that there's more to
life than I ever imagined

LULU FERRAND

Story Terrace

StoryTerrace

www.StoryTerrace.com

Dedicated to all those starting out on their spiritual journey

CONTENTS

INTRODUCTION

Yesterday is history
Tomorrow a mystery
And today is a gift
That's why it's called
'The present'
– Kung Fu Panda

This is the story of ten years in my life when I have learnt so much and come an incredibly long way. I am just not the same person. At the beginning, I am emotionally detached (the only way to get through Western cancer treatment), money-driven and socially impressed by rank.

But I am now aware of how we as humans have not developed the way that was intended. For generations, we have evolved, surrounding ourselves with jealousy, greed and violence. And the most important lesson we haven't learnt is not to fear death. My eyes are now open to what we are here on the Earth to learn, and why we keep coming back to continue that learning. This happens during a process called reincarnation.

The Latin definition of the word reincarnation is 'entering the flesh again.' We all seem to have differing beliefs about whether reincarnation actually exists. Certainly, the different religious sects cannot agree either. I have ignored what religions have declared; after all, religions are man-made anyway. Most Christian and Islamic faiths do not believe in reincarnation. Most Indian religions, such as Hinduism, Buddhism and Sikhism, do believe in reincarnation. I have asked myself what I believe from my own experiences, and I have decided that I believe in reincarnation from what I have experienced personally and within my treatment room. My answer to this question comes from within and I do not need to have proof. If you do need evidence, then read Dr Jim Tucker's books. He is a researcher from the University of West Virginia and reports on case studies of children's past lives. I will leave it up to him to prove to you.

We are here on Earth to learn to love one another, to connect with our inner self and trust that everything we need is right here within us. When we have fully learned that, then we can describe ourselves as successful. I consider myself successful. I am not rich, I have no ego, I do not fear death, and I love everyone and everything on this earth. This is the story of my journey, which I am still on, learning something new every day I live on this planet.

A brief introduction to the main characters in my book...

Lulu (that's me) – diagnosed with breast cancer six months before the beginning of this diary. Divorced a man called Perry when her children were 12 and 14 years old. She makes her living selling stationery and is especially proud of the beautiful leather-bound diaries she sells. She was raised on a farm by down-to-earth and loving parents. Brought up a Christian but has no religious beliefs to speak of. Her favourite food is lasagne because it's the one thing she cooks that everyone loves.

Richard Ferrand – boyfriend who was briefly married for four years. Subsequently, is traumatised by films about love. Generally emotionally restrained, dyslexic and a party animal. Loves people and being the centre of attention. Looks like an ageing rocker from the '80s. Bossy but fragile underneath.

Alice Littleboy, sensitive, cries easily but tough and determined underneath. Fun to be with, always has a story and is the one you need to be near.

Digby Littleboy, quiet, driven, worries about others before himself. 'Dad' sense of humour, dry.

Jamie Ferrand – hardworking, kind and has a strong relationship with Dad, Richard.

Ed Theakston - yes, the brewing family. Lifelong friend of Lulu's.

Mancy Cobb - lifelong friend and Alice's Godmother. Lives in a large house in Putney. Married with three children. Calm and quietly driven.

The world is my country, all mankind are my brethren, and to do good is my religion.
– Thomas Paine

I USED TO BE NORMAL

Lulu

1. DIARY

The choice to seek, to awaken the spiritual self, is, of course, free to each person on this planet and to each person in this whole universe. Not everyone is going to realise it.
– Bringers of the Dawn by Barbara Marciniak

In order for you to truly understand the journey I have taken, let's begin in 2011. This is where it all started, when I discovered the power of self-healing and much more...

01.01.11 Lots of 1s in today's date and what a strange day it was. Lesley (my Manual Lymphatic Drainage massage therapist) lent me a book – Reiki for Beginners. I told her last week that I was interested in Reiki and how people learned how to do it. Richard was pheasant shooting for the day, so I had a peaceful time on my own. Just after lunch, it could have been 11 minutes past one (didn't make a note of the time), whilst reading the chapter about individual Reiki Masters and their stories, I felt a buzzing all over my body. It felt as if I was being given a treatment. As if I have been plugged into the national grid. It's not a scary feeling, quite comforting really, more of a healing sort of energy. I have no idea what it is, but it is still with me several hours later.

02.01.11 The buzzing is still here and woke me several times during the night. I struggled to find somewhere to put my hands because when my hands are on my body, the buzzing intensified dramatically. No point seeing a doctor, this is something he wouldn't know about. Feel that it is doing something really good though.

04.01.11 We arrived at Ed and Vanda Theakston's house last night and today I stay in bed for the first part of the morning. I still have the Reiki book with me and Lesley's business card as a bookmark. It kept on falling out of the book and onto my lap, three times in all and finally, I noticed the chapter where the card was – Self-Healing. Mmmmm, very interesting. The funny thing is, it feels as if it is working. I alternate my hands from hips up to my head and then vice versa. Don't want it to build up energy and then stagnate so I try to keep moving my hands around my body. I am sure I have more vitality this evening.

I think back to last November when I decided to go to church, having not been since the previous Christmas. I sat at the back with my turban covering my bald head and listened to the sermon. It was all about healing and she ended the sermon with 'Go out and heal.' Jane, the vicar, apologised as I left, for delivering a sermon about healing when I have been in and out of hospitals over the past few months. I said 'Don't worry, I think it's a sign.'

08.01.11 Up until now, I have been having an afternoon nap. I have been feeling utterly exhausted and it was the only way to keep on an even keel, strength-wise. During the past few days that I have been practising my self-healing Reiki techniques, I really have had a boost. I practise twice a day and no longer need sleep in the afternoons. Richard is being extremely strict and making me go to bed. I am telling him some of what is going on with me, but he is very uncomfortable about it.

10.01.11 Started radiotherapy today and worried that it may stop my buzzy energy flow. After my first session it seems to be fine, and the buzzing is still with me. I notice that if I put my hands in my groin (such a horrid word) I can feel a pulling up and to under my arms. It seems to be the lymph system sorting itself out, good stuff, wayhay!

Today I decide that I need to learn more about my body and the healing I seem to have acquired because I am absolutely sure I can help others. I don't want to be a wacky healer but would like some sort of qualification and training to be a healer that might tempt all the waverers and sceptics to give it a go. I'd like to change their attitudes.

So, after some research on the internet and talking with the course director, I decide to embark on a Biodynamic Craniosacral therapy course. What a mouthful – I will probably just end up calling myself a healer in the end! I did mention my buzz but the course director didn't pick up on it, and I didn't push it. Maybe it's something everyone who heals has.

I'd had a treatment on a recent holiday in Florida; my friend who I was staying with won it in a raffle and gave it to me. I was blown away.

The practitioner uses light touch on various parts of the body in order to tune into the nervous system. By doing this, emotional or physical trauma held in the tissues can be released. So, it is possible to release birth trauma in a 70-year-old! Being a human, we experience stress, injury and trauma and this can get stored in the tissues either physically or as a memory. CST can allow the body to let all this go, bit like a reset. My experience in Florida included bones straightening, voices in my head saying, 'It's ok to be on my own,' stretching, fizzing and aching and after it, I felt reborn. I just had to learn how to do this for myself. Anyway, the course just seems the right thing to do, I'm listening to my gut.

Before I can begin the course proper though, I need to know something about the human body. With not even an O-level in biology, this is a huge gap in my knowledge, so I also decide to sign up to the Living Anatomy and Physiology course – the 'school' is called Craniosacral Therapy Educational Trust – CTET for short. The first seminar is at the end of this month.

What a day! Feel very positive and I know I am heading in the right direction. Probably for the first time in my life. "I feel good, du nu nu nu nur, so good, so fine!" It's extraordinary that in under three weeks, I have changed the direction of my life.

18.01.11 Still doing my radiotherapy treatments each day but more importantly doing regular self-healing (twice a day). Wish I was brave enough to stop the radiotherapy. Sometimes the energy buzz is so overpowering I have to take my hands off my body, but it seems to be doing its stuff because I am feeling much better.

24.01.11 Went to see Ralph, a spiritual healer, whom I have been seeing over the past few months and told him all about the signs and buzzing in my body. He seemed quite excited about it. He told me not to get cocky, that I was a channel for healing and more will be coming my way, maybe clairvoyance! Woaah! That sounds wacky! He says my guide is an ancient Japanese man – can't remember his name – must ask him next time. Weird stuff though. I decide I will use Ralph as my mentor as I really believe I can do the healing myself. Definitely can't tell Richard this!

Have decided to up my self-healing to three times a day: two reasons – one, I am feeling so much better and two, I am actually really enjoying it. It feels like time out for me.

25.01.11 Still doing the radiotherapy. Got there early and phoned my sister, Daphne, from the car in the car park. She was complaining of a headache. We chatted about her over-indulgence the night before and about some of the weird stuff happening to me and by the end of the phone call, her headache had gone. Really not keen on healing self-inflicted ailments though!

29.01.11 First weekend of Living Anatomy and Physiology course. We sit in a semicircle on bean bags and chairs, fifteen of us, and we have to introduce ourselves and say a little about why we are here. How nerve-wracking – I hate being the centre of attention. I don't mind talking to one or two but to a crowd, I am really out of my comfort zone. Luckily, I have a bottle of 'Rescue Remedy', marvellous stuff, in my handbag; I have a good few pipettes full. Gradually it comes to my turn and by the time I am the next one, my heart is pounding. I manage to give my outline.

'My name is Lulu and I live in Leicestershire with my partner, Richard. I have two children and one stepson. I was living a normal life until I was diagnosed with (big breath) breast cancer. As you can see (big breath again) I have gone through chemotherapy and am currently in the middle of four weeks of radiotherapy. Something happened to me on the first of January this year and my body went buzzy – still is buzzing – and I am being drawn towards healing. I don't want to be a wacky healer, I want to do proper training. But before I do that I need to know about the human body. That's why I'm here.'

I did it! Thank goodness it's over. I nearly cracked but held it together, thanks to the RR. Ugh, I absolutely hate doing that kind of thing.

'Thank you for sharing that with us' says the tutor, Sarah Nesling.

I feel the tension leave my body, at least I won't have to do that again. I was surprised though, that no one came to me afterwards to tell me what this buzzy feeling is.

I decided to stay in a hotel rather than with friends, it adds to the cost but means that I can lie on my bed, close my eyes, heal myself and recharge my battery. Which means I can get through the next day. It's hurting my brain which hasn't been used for learning for a couple of decades.

Fascinating learning about the body and I really enjoyed the weekend. But one thing was really annoying me: I am missing out on what happens at the weekends. We have parties and dinners on these weekends that are booked; all my socialising happens at home at the weekends. The course is only once every 6 weeks and with homework in between but I have to say no to the parties and let Richard go on his own. Feel as if I am really missing out. But get real, girl – I haven't the energy to do it anyway, at the moment.

31.01.11 Radiotherapy, as usual, at 9 a.m. When I return home, Digby is sitting in the snug looking sheepish. He tearfully tells me he has crashed his beloved Land Rover which he owns with two other friends and was planning on driving through Africa with. He'd crashed into a poor lady in a Ka just a few miles away from home as he was pulling out of a junction. The Ka lady is taken in an ambulance to hospital with minor injuries. He is also very worried about letting his friends down. Thank goodness Richard was here to take charge because Digby is in shock.

Have been noticing my self-healing buzzing feeling is not very strong in the mornings and evenings but mid-afternoon it is powerful. Maybe because I feel more relaxed when lying on my bed having my afternoon nap. Or maybe the healing is stronger when I am at my weakest.

Richard is really nagging me about resting to manage my energy levels. I don't argue because I love the hands-on energising feeling I am getting. It's like a drug, I'm getting hooked on it!

This afternoon is one of those powerful ones. I notice colours behind my eyes; bright pink and lime green alternating in waves. My tinnitus is heightened, very loud at times. When I have my hands over my head and eyes, I 'see' a fabulous neon light display for approximately two minutes with tubules of bright blue light shooting from the outside into the black middle and disappearing into the black hole in the centre. Great stuff but I don't know what the heck is going on. Oh well, enjoy the show.

That evening Digby rings the Ka lady to apologise, she was short with him, but he thinks it was appreciated. I know the insurance companies don't like you to admit it was your fault, but it's just good manners. He has recently passed his test and pulled out without properly checking, she was in a 30 zone and going downhill with a parked car obstructing the view. Digby thinks over the speed limit but nevertheless, he should not have pulled out. He definitely feels better after the call.

01.02.11 Digby gets news from the garage that they are going to write off the Land Rover. Mainly because it is not worth very much but to Digby it is worth a lot – and to his two friends. They had been getting it ready for a road trip to South Africa for which they couldn't get insurance, so the route changed to southern Europe. A fridge, tent, camping kit and subwoofers (very important) had been fitted ready for the imminent trip. So today's write-off news was a blow. The friends were very understanding and said that it could have happened to any one of them. They then began searching for another vehicle on the internet that they could buy with the insurance money which, I am sure, would have been an even bigger heap of junk. I put my foot down and despairingly said 'Someone is trying to tell you something, do not go on a road trip. Buy backpacks and do it like everyone else!' After a ring round, the other parents agreed with me. Sometimes you just have to listen to what is going on around you.

It does worry me that teenagers are plugged into gadgets most of the day and are losing their connection to reality.

07.02.11 Last day of radiotherapy. It doesn't seem to have taken away any of my buzzy energy. Even when I am sitting at the computer and not thinking about healing, I feel its presence.

09.02.11 A Traveller came to visit. I didn't let her in because Richard was not here; I kept her on the doorstep. She said that I needed to get out more because someone with an R in their name was going to be very important to me and to be careful of someone with an M in their name as they were jealous of me. She got the R bit right, not sure about who the M could be. But the most interesting thing was that she said I had received a gift and that I should use it. She also said that one of my children has this gift too. Not quite so good news was the fact that I would never be rich: rich inside, yes, but not materially rich.

Heard Jessie J's new song on the radio, *It's not about the money, money, money…* and keep singing it for the rest of the day. How true is that?!

12.02.11 Richard and I travel up to Newcastle for the weekend to see Alice. Jamie, my stepson, and Digby join us too. Alice is having the time of her life at Uni, not sure how much work she is doing at the moment though. Interesting the comparison to my late learning and how keen I am to glean more: completely different from when I was at school when I was less interested than Alice.

We stay in a hotel and before dinner I have my usual recharge. The buzz is still going, raging at times but I can't manage without it. I really love it, whatever it is. Whilst I am 'resting' Richard manages to chat up a local blond at the bar. He is 'full of it' for the rest of the evening, he says that at his age he can still pull the chicks! The children find this hilarious. We go out for dinner with about 25 of Alice's friends for her 21st birthday, have to rein Richard back and stop him from clubbing! He's really too old for all this!

15.02.11 I go to the Leicester Lymphoedema clinic to get rechecked for the swelling in my hand. She tells me once you have it, you have it for life. Absolutely not! I will not spend the rest of my life wearing a glove and sleeve to prevent swelling. I feel that news is worse than the cancer (which, by the way, I do not have any more!). I tell her of my MLD (Manual

Lymphatic Drainage) therapist and the techniques I am using like brushing my skin to train the body to use other lymph nodes. I do it several times a day and will not be beaten on this. A new friend, Helen, who has lymphoedema warned me of it. Hers is quite bad and she said if she had known what she does now and acted straight away then she thought she would not have a problem. She told me about Lesley, the MLD therapist, and I am very grateful. I'm going to crack it though.

17.02.11 Still doing the brushing techniques for the lymphoedema and putting my left hand under my right armpit during my recharge sessions. It is very buzzy and I am absolutely sure it is having an effect.

18.02.11 Religiously doing my clearing and brushing techniques to train my lymph system. I am looking forward to learning more about the lymph system on my course.

An extraordinary recharge session this afternoon. I closed my eyes and saw a tall man and a shorter man standing side by side, only their bodies and above, no legs showing. Don't know who they are or what it means.

22.02.11 Digby and his friends have been planning a trip to South America. He has spent the last six months working all hours to save up. Some of his hard-earned cash went on the shortfall in insurance payout to his co-owners but he should still manage. The trip to South America is a few weeks off but they are still determined to 'do' Europe, Amsterdam being a highlight. So they are off today with the newly purchased backpack!

During this afternoon's recharge when I closed my eyes, I saw a table with people sitting all around it. In the darkness behind my eyes, the shape I saw was a light greeny colour. It is impossible to make out the people or whether they were male or female but they were of different sizes, with a more prominent one in the foreground. I've booked an appointment with Ralph, maybe he can tell me what's going on.

23.02.11 Spoke to Franklyn Sills, who runs the Karuna Institute in Devon, and seems to be the guru in the Craniosacral world. I explained my buzzy feelings and asked him what was happening. He said he wasn't sure! Can't believe that? Surely healing people should know what this is. It must happen to others, I can't be the only one.

Also spoke with a tutor, from CTET (Craniosacral Therapy Educational Trust), who has a similar response. The two courses are very similar except Karuna is residential and seems to be better hours. I hate disrupting my weekends, I don't know how others do it. I do have a life!

24.02.11 Mark Lomas, a very close friend of Richards, who used to live in our flat, now lives in the next village. He has a wacky sister-in-law who is over from America and so we go over to Mark's for a drink. She refers to herself as a healer so I was thrilled to be able to talk about what's happening to me with someone who doesn't think I've gone a bit odd! She told me to slow down! Ralph told me that too last month! I am naturally impatient though. She said I would be guided and to write a journal because some amazing things will happen on my journey. She said to look for my own way of doing things and not necessarily follow the Craniosacral way. Oh wow, this is all so amazing. I tell Richard snippets but not too much detail; need to break him in gently, he finds this way too weird for him.

26.02.11 The second Living Anatomy weekend course and I'm really looking forward to it.

We sit in our semi-circle again and I notice a few new faces that weren't there the weekend before. Sarah Nesling opens the day with a little meditation to settle us all down. Meditation is new to me; in the 'odd zone' of the past but I really enjoy them. The buzz is always very strong during a meditation. Maybe that's what I've been doing anyway, in my rest time!

Then to my horror, she says that as there are three new people we should say a little about ourselves all over again. My Rescue Remedy is over the other side of the room and not at all handy!

I calmed myself with the thought that I'd done it before and managed it then, so this time I should be ok. It came towards my turn and my heart was racing. I began and the first few words flowed, all was going well. But when I had to say the word CANCER, I cracked. I cried but carried on with the little speech, sobbing between words. Sarah said I could stop but I felt it was important for my body to release it. I struggled to the end and felt a huge relief. My immediate trauma was released but I am sure there's more in there. It seems pushed down below my diaphragm and that's how I describe being able to cope, with my hands in a pushing-down motion.

The rest of the weekend goes well, learning about cells, which is a bit, no, a lot, over my head. I am letting it all wash over me because I am sure it'll make sense in the end.

28.02.11 Ralph tells me to slow down again! Slow down, not really sure what he means. Maybe I am just being too hungry to learn more and I should let it happen when it wants to happen. I tell him of the shapes I have seen behind my eyes, of the two people, one tall and one small. He tells me they are my spiritual guides who are looking after me – wooah! He also tells me that the taller one is the one to follow and not so much the smaller one as 'it' is not as clever. This feels blasphemous almost and I feel very uncomfortable. I think Ralph feels this way too. We also discuss the people sitting around a table, he doesn't know what is happening there or what the message is. I am definitely not telling Richard this stuff!

5-19.03.11 Lou and Chris Davies, very close friends, have an apartment in Mauritius. They have given it to us for a couple of weeks, we just have to pay for flights. I couldn't think of a better place to go to fully recuperate. How lucky we are. We spend more on the flight and go Economy Plus, after all, I am still not firing on 6 cylinders. I wear an extra sleeve and glove on my right arm, but I am determined not to wear it on the beach. I'll do lots of swimming and keep it at bay.

It turns out to be the most fabulous place: two bedrooms, two bathrooms, gorgeous sitting room/dining room. And on the balcony was a plunge pool, another dining table for eight and two sun loungers. I am so grateful to be in such a wonderful place to fully recuperate.

The first morning I look at the infinity pool and decide I shall swim four times a day and do ten lengths each time, not too much. And in the evenings, I am going to walk around the golf course, the first nine holes only. My target should be easy enough to do with all the lazing around on sun beds in between…

Glove and sleeve abandoned in the apartment, I begin my first length. Towards the other end of the pool, I realise I wasn't going to make much more. The chemo and radiotherapy had taken their toll and I should give in and let my body restore itself. Although irritated that my target didn't seem achievable, I got over it because it meant I could spend my days on a fabulous double bed with wicker sides and lots of cushions underneath a palm tree, interspersed with a little swimming and eating. My arm did prickle at times and I used that as my cue to get in the water with the motion of the water dispersing the lymph buildup.

Laying during the day on the sunbed was wonderfully resourceful. I lay there doing my self-healing, working up and down my body and soaking in the sun. I didn't care who saw me. I also abandoned my turban as I have almost ¾ of an inch on my head. I think I look quite chic with short hair.

My energy begins to restore and after a week of this, I am beginning to feel like my old self again. The battery seems fuller and I start attacking those lengths and by the end of the holiday I had managed to stride the first nine holes of the golf course.

'I feel good, du nu nu nu nur'

20.03.11 We get back home feeling refreshed. Richard hadn't realised how much energy and vitality he had lost during these past traumatic few months. My hair grew quite a bit whilst we were away and the glove and sleeve have been discarded completely, though if I play tennis, I will certainly put it on.

I am feeling enormously grateful and thankful, so I have been planning how to show my appreciation to all my friends who supported me while going through this ordeal. I would have a small bash for my Essex girls and a bigger one for everyone else. The invitations go out.

23.03.11 Having a bit of a 'life is too short' feeling today. Spend the day planning a family holiday which has so far been a rarity because there are always more important things to spend our money on. And now they are adults in the travel world dictionary means that they are full fare and therefore the cost of a holiday equates to a small extension on the house. But I feel it is something that we must, must do. And it shows we are a unit. Maybe Richard will propose to me when we are there, would be perfect as we are all together. Forget the proposing, maybe he'll marry me on a white beach and we'll have all of us there. I get rid of that thought because I don't feel he is ready for commitment yet. One day... maybe...

30.03.11 My Essex girlfriends come up and we have lunch in the Fox and Hounds, paid for by me. I do a little speech about how special they are and how I wouldn't have recovered so well without them. They are my nearest and dearest friends from my 'previous' life and where I lived whilst being married.

When my marriage of 18 years went 'skew whiff', I decided to move to Leicestershire and start afresh. Some thought me mad but it felt right at the time and again I listened to my gut. If I hadn't moved, I wouldn't have met Richard, about whom I am totally besotted. But the all-important support network when illness raises its ugly head was not there, or so I thought. Lots of local acquaintances came out of the woodwork and I realised that I do have a support network locally too: and more importantly, they became my friends.

05.04.11 My birthday. Digby comes back and tells lots of stories about his trip. I surmise they are heavily censored because the lovely leather travel diary I gave him to fill in doesn't leave his side. I don't suppose I will ever find out. Nothing more than I did! I hope!

No proposal today. Would have been perfect timing as we are having the party in May, which would save on the expense of an engagement party.

10.04.11 The Ka lady is going to sue for damages. Luckily the insurance company is sorting it all out. It really was an 'accident' in the true sense of the word. Still, it leaves a sour taste when I read the list of what she is claiming for, including psychotherapy. I bet she has been contacted by a no-win-no-fee lawyer. Even Digby received a call from a shark lawyer.

12.04.11 Digby is off on his South America travels and back at the beginning of August, just before our big family holiday to Thailand.

After all the swimming in Mauritius and feeling so good, I decided to continue it. I don't actually like swimming, or should I say I don't like the getting dressed and smelling of chlorine for the rest of the day.

However, our local swimming pool is salt water and the getting dressed bit is not so bad after all. Swimming is such good exercise, keeping me supple and the lymph moving.

28.04.11 Another session with Ralph, nothing really to report but he did say that his healing abilities are going to a new level. I feel as if mine are too. Time to put them into practice!

Richard has been complaining of tennis elbow. He doesn't actually play that much tennis; maybe it's from all the computer work he does. I have kept him in the dark about much of what has been going on with me on a spiritual level. It's bedtime and he's reading The Week, which seems to take him a week to read; I am sure that's not what it's all about! I suggested I just put my hands on his elbow and let's just see what happens. I can feel the tissues twanging and moving about between my hands.

'Ow, ow, ow what are you doing?' Richard says.

'I'm not doing anything; it's your body having a sort out, I promise I'm not doing anything. Do you want me to stop?'

'No, keep doing it.'

It reduced in intensity the longer I held his elbow. After about ten minutes, I stopped. It felt a bit sore. Oops.

29.04.11 Richard's tennis elbow seems to have gone! Not seems to have, *has* gone! Wow, wow, wow.

It's the Royal Wedding today and we celebrate it with Juliet and Mark, friends in Essex, and we travel south for the day. We pretend we are there in Westminster Abbey and sing along, all wearing hats! Really good fun. Richard returns north and I stay down south because of my annoying course happening on weekends and I will commute in tomorrow.

30.04.11 Alice and Jamie have a whole bunch of friends coming to stay and there's a street party in the village. And I'm stuck in London doing this course. Actually, when I'm there I really enjoy it but it's irritating that I am missing out again.

15.05.11 Today is my 'Hats Off party!' It was a lunch for 50 in a marquee on the lawn. It's my way of thanking everyone. The Essex gang comes with their husbands and all the others are locals, family from Yorkshire, new friends and old ones – all those who went out of their way to support me. Everyone has to wear a hat, at least for the first bit before sitting down. I start a speech and tell them of an article in the paper recently about social wealth. This is the amount of support around you, the network of family and friends. Social wealth is vital if you come across a disaster. I told them with the social wealth I had, I should be a millionaire. They all cheered. I wore a bright pink bob wig: the only wig I ever bought, no point trying to hide the fact! Thought I'd laugh in the face of it. At the end of the speech, I grab hold of it and fling it in the air — all the guests fling their hats too. So we have the air full of flat hats, top hats, baseball caps, even a pith helmet!

Each napkin has a label with a handwritten personal message from me thanking them for their bit. They all took them home. It took me ages to write them but I didn't want to miss anyone out in my speech and anyway, it would be way too many thank yous for them to sit through.

It was a really special day; so warm and loving with the most amazing atmosphere, and all those people got the thanks they deserved. I absolutely loved it.

26.05.11 When I'm at the checkout till at Tesco, it crashes. That's the second time that has happened. Is it me?

04.06.11 Richard decides to clean the garage door with the hosepipe and a long-handled brush. He really goes for it, scrubbing up and down. For someone who takes very little exercise and never visits a gym this is perhaps not the wisest thing to do. The inevitable happens and he pulls a muscle, behind his shoulder blade (probably the trapezius, anatomy getting better!). He comes rushing in looking very sorry for himself and asks me to put my hands on him. Now this is a real breakthrough in his acknowledging that some sort of healing happens. I put my hands on him, there was a little bit of 'Ow, owing' but then after about five minutes, the tissues stopped moving, I took my hands away and the pain disappeared.

My desire to heal the world is very strong and I have to stop myself from thinking that I may be the next Dalai Lama or Florence Nightingale. There is a feeling of being something special, though. Dying to start the Craniosacral course in October, it can't come soon enough. Oh, I forgot, slow down. Nag, nag.

05.06.11 I am noticing a new very faint buzz in my body, down my spine, I think. The main buzz of energy is still there but there is an intermittent other buzz too. I think it might be my parasympathetic nervous system kicking in and I can switch it on and off. Very strange but we are studying it at the moment – is my body showing me?

11.06.11 The course again this weekend. It's my friend Diana's 50th tonight. It's a big party with dinner and dancing and I am afraid I draw the line at missing that, so I ask for the day off on the Sunday and catch up later. I did make the Saturday, so it's not that bad.

14.06.11 I start playing tennis again. I knock up gently for about five minutes in the service box to let my arm prepare itself for what is about to happen. I wear my sleeve and glove. It's great to get back on the court again and by the end of the set my arm feels a little sore but there is no lymph fluid swelling.

15.06.11 I go to the post office to send a parcel for a Scribble House customer of mine. When I get to the counter, the terminal crashes. He has to turn it off, wait and then on again. I wonder if it's me. It might be.

20.06.11 No one on my course seems to feel the same buzz, I mention it to the tutors and it falls on deaf ears. No one seems to know what it is.

So today I spent hours searching on the internet to see if others have felt what I am feeling. In my search, I discover a man called James Oschman who is a professor and came through the scientific route and now is a specialist in energy medicine. He spoke at the Breath of Life Conference in London, so I order a disc of his lecture. He also has contributed to a DVD called The Living Matrix, which is all about energy in the body. I order them both. I might be on the right track.

22.06.11 The Living Matrix DVD arrives and I immediately watch it. No answers there.

23.06.11 Professor James Oschman's CD arrives, again I sit down and watch it straight away. It is very interesting, I think I'm getting warmer. He talks of jet lag, if you travel abroad, when you arrive at your destination, take off your shoes and let yourself be grounded by the Earth – made a mental note to try it on our trip to Thailand. At the end, he asks the audience how many people can hear their nervous system. Maybe that's my buzz; it's my nervous system. As the camera is fixed on him I don't see the display of hands. So, I write to the Professor himself.

Dear Professor Oschman,
Re: your lecture at the Breath of Life Conference.
I totally 'get' what you are saying, it all makes perfect sense. I was wondering how many people put up their hands when you asked the question as to whether they could hear their nervous system. The CD didn't show the audience. I would have put up my hand; I hear it most of the time! Not only that, I have another sensation when I am stressed, a deeper tighter frequency buzz which I can stop by setting off the parasympathetic nervous system (I presume). And when I get too 'buzzy', I take off my shoes – some shoes are worse than others. I haven't always been able to hear it, a recent acquisition.

So, what I would like to know is your plan for lectures/workshops over the coming year. If not in the UK, then I may just have to wait for two years' time. I am doing the Living Anatomy course run by the CTET and in October start the Craniosacral training proper.
Yours sincerely,
Lulu Littleboy

The reply came back the same day. I am impressed because he is a busy man.

Dear Lulu,
Thank you for your note. I am grateful to Jane for passing your email on to me. And thank you for your comments about my presentation. I do not remember how many people put their hands up when I asked if they can hear the sound of their nervous system. I actually discovered this for myself many years ago, and was happy to learn that my friend, John Beaulieu, has been researching this for years.
He then lists his schedule dates and concludes with:
I do hope we will meet up at one of these events.
Thanks again,
Jim

I was disappointed; I expected a bit more of a reply than that. I'm not sure I am on the right track after all. I thought he might ask me more about it and what I was feeling but he was very matter-of-fact. My stuff going on is not matter-of-fact. I'll keep at it.

24.06.11 I offer some 'hands on' to Alice, who is back for a week before going to London to look for a job. She is feeling tired and needed a pep-up. I thought I would just give her some energy. She lay across the end of her double bed and I knelt at the side and put my hands on her shoulders. 'Oooh, it feels tingly, Mummy,' and she lay there and relaxed. She then suddenly cried out with a loud and welling 'ughha' then promptly burst into tears. She said it was freaky, and she had a light that she felt coming up her body and filling her head. I took my hands away.

I now know that she is the child with the same gift; she has to be. It wasn't freaky, it was a special moment, but she didn't seem ready to accept it.

29.06.11 Life feels normal again. I am playing tennis twice a week, thinking of expanding my leather stationery business and going to rock concerts! Saw Bon Jovi, Rod Stewart and Take That at Hyde Park in four nights over last weekend. I'm such a cool Mum! And normal! There's nothing strange about me!

I signed up for The Rutland Tennis Tournament, which is this Sunday. It's my focus because I will feel as if I'm completely back to normal.

03.07.11 Tennis tournament day. I get knocked out in the semi-finals! Wayhay! Not bad for someone who was so crook!

08.07.11 A weekend in Thorpeness with Juliet and Mark Ballamy of Essex days. They are very dear friends and have a stunning house there on the Mere. Extras were invited for Saturday night and I sat next to David Gamble, a business angel from Cambridge who has a holiday cottage in Aldeburgh. It was fascinating talking to him about his latest venture. He is investing in a research project on the mind/body connection. It will take twenty years and the first ten will be spent building a computerised human so that experiments can be done in the second decade. Well done! I told him how I'd been feeling this year and that there's definitely more to the human body than we in the Western world have taken into account. The East seems so in tune with the energy and spiritual connection. It is so exciting that something is being done within our medical world. I promise to send him the DVDs of James Oschman and The Living Matrix.

16.07.11 Another weekend of the course. It happens about every five weeks, and in between, there is homework and reading. And I'm really loving it. I eagerly look forward to these weekends and no longer resent what I am missing out on. The balance of importance has changed, which has rather shocked me. Most unlike me, totally out of character, but I actually don't mind what I am missing at home now; I'd rather be learning about the body.

I have been noticing that whatever we are studying, I start feeling it in my body. The other day I looked up the adrenal glands because I had forgotten what they produced, and above my kidneys were popping as if someone was flicking it with a finger; they were alternating, one and then the other. I laughed out loud; 'I know where they are, I just need to know what they do!'

29.07.11 Another treatment from Ralph. I tell him of the checkout tills and ask if it could be something to do with the amount of energy in me. He says it probably is because he has the same problem. I also reported to him that I haven't seen any shapes, my two guides or many colours behind my eyes for months. That bit was true, but rather naughtily and not because I really believed it, I tell him that I was wondering whether my guides had changed their minds and decided that I am not worthy or good enough.

At that moment, I rub my eye; I'm not sure why because it didn't itch, but behind my eyes is a person shape, bright red pinky in colour. I tell Ralph and then double-check by closing my eyes again – the man/woman is still there. Ralph assures me that my guides are still there supporting me on my journey. Wow! That was incredible. That was a huge moment. Now I really believe that they are there for me. A big step on the ladder of my spiritual journey. I am humbled as I drive away. I feel confident and not alone. I tell Richard, who thinks it is all way too odd, this may be the last thing I tell him. If he thinks I'm too strange he may just up and go.

03.08.11 I go to London to have my interview with a Tutor of the Biodynamic Craniosacral Therapy course. I feel as if it is more me interviewing him rather than the other way around. Is it really the right course? I quiz him about energy and he assures me it is a form of energy healing. So, I decide to enrol.

It starts on the 19th October and I can't wait. I decide that I will use it as a framework because other stuff seems to be being given to me. So, I shall be using my gut instinct as well and a little help from above. Now that I believe there is something up there and that when I die it's not the end, it has given me a warm and comfortable feeling. I feel quietly confident with no fear of death at all. But thinking about it, the no fear of dying has been building up over the past few months and has come upon me gradually. I feel wholesome and good.

'I feel good, du nu nu nu nur...'

I am also wondering if everyone has some sort of ability to self-heal, just at different levels, a bit like being able to paint. We can all do it, but some can do it more easily than others.

05.08.11 We set off for a family holiday in Thailand. Digby was delayed from his trip and made it just in time with only a few hours to clean his grubby clothes. So having realised that life is too short and we should make the most of it, we raided the savings pot and spent it on a once-in-a-lifetime holiday. I want an adventure with the children.

Alice is now job hunting after having just finished reading Politics. She got a 2:1 which meant that she worked harder than I thought, though perhaps just in her final year. Her first year was a different story; she hardly even went to a lecture but preferred the party life. She is pretty and blond as well as fun and sensible – a great combination.

Digby, my gorgeous son, the one who causes the most angst, has always wanted to be a chef. He wanted to leave school after GCSEs, but his father and I insisted he should get his A-levels. He may change his mind about his cooking career and anyway, you solidify your friends between 16 and 18 so it was important to stay. He has just had his 19th birthday and will start his chef's training in September at Westminster College. His expectations are high; I think he will find it a difficult career choice, always working when everyone else is having fun at weekends. But I can understand a passion because that's what I am feeling about my course now. I have never felt passionate about anything before. I'm 48 and could have done so much already if I'd managed to work out what my career should be. Selling stationery never felt right, especially when I don't like selling.

Jamie is Richard's son and the one I feel I have acquired. I am the chief negotiator in the father/son relationship and smooth the waters. They get on well, but Richard has a tendency to be overly strict, but then he says I am too soft. I believe in boundaries and am soft until the boundary is crossed and then I come down like a ton of bricks – and the kids know it.

Jamie is passionate about flying and passed his PPL when he was 17. He qualified before he passed his driving test, so there was much hilarity in the fact that he could fly but couldn't actually drive to the airport!

What is amazing is we all get on so well, my put-together new family. What a blessing.

On the plane, I am planning how and where to do the grounding thing of taking off my shoes. I am looking forward to giving it a go.

We land and head for the passport queue; the boys go to another queue, several queues away thinking it shorter. Alice and I wait in the nearest one. It's a good thing the boys are further away because I plan to do my grounding experiment in the queue. The boys are all very closed to what is happening to me and almost shut down when anything out of the ordinary is related. Alice is more in touch with her body and open to possibilities. I warn her about what I am about to do – she is comfortable with it.

I discreetly slip off my shoes, and with my bare feet on the cold stone floor, I close my eyes and relax. I begin to feel the energy flow up my left leg, across my pelvis and then up my right side. This feels amazing and lasts a couple of minutes, and then seems to balance itself. Wow! Must remember to email James Oschman and tell him about it. Horses don't get jet-lagged; in fact, they are energised when they travel. It must be their metal shoes! They contact the Earth when they land and are grounded! Maybe I'm onto something here, but surely others have thought about it.

We have three days in Bangkok and do the usual tours. The Grand Palace is an outstanding place with several gold temples. It feels very strong energetically but it's also a very hot day. We go into the temple with the emerald Buddha in it and I feel compelled to kneel down with the locals. Wow, there's a strong energy here. I close my eyes and feel it coming up from the Earth and all around me. So strong that I almost fall over but stop myself just in time. I'm moved – in more ways than one...

We go to Chiang Mai for a few days and spent a day at an elephant farm, "owning" an elephant for the day. We had to feed, wash, walk and ride them. We rode them to a waterfall so we could swim with them in it. Richard and I refrained; it was very grubby water, too grubby for me with my immune system possibly not up to full efficiency, and Richard can't swim, so not a good exercise for him!

As Richard climbed off the elephant, his back had gone into spasm and he was in agony. He really had not enjoyed this experience. We stood on the edge of the waterfall, looking down at the elephants below, with my hands on his back. After a few minutes, the pain went away. Unfortunately, I then had a back problem. I must work out this grounding business because it was sore for several days and Richard was fine.

Richard and Jamie went fishing for the day and Digby went on a cooking course. Alice and I had a trip planned to Tao Garden which is a health spa run by Mantak Chia, who is a Grand Master of the Tao. Tao is the natural order of the universe, the path, the road; the proper way of being in existence. An energetic way of being whilst in harmony with nature and the universe. I like the sound of that!

I really wanted to meet Mantak Chia and ask him about what has been happening to me. We have booked several treatments throughout the day. We were greeted at reception and informed of the timings of our treatments. We were warned that one of the treatments I had booked for Alice, Karsai Nei Tsang Detox Therapy, involved not only an abdominal massage but also an internal one! Alice decided that she would miss out the internal bit. We met after the massage and I asked her how it went and she told me that when it came to the internal bit she told the Thai masseur to 'go ahead' and she replied 'Good for boyfriend, good for boyfriend'! She doesn't have a boyfriend at the moment. We laughed a lot!

I had colonic irrigation; we both had our auras done and chakras read. What an amazing place. The lunch had labels referring to what blood groups should eat what. Some of the guests looked as if they needed major healing. Perhaps this is a last resort place when you've tried everything else. I certainly would book myself in if I felt crook. I feel I would trust them over and above the Western doctors. They said I had a gallbladder problem and gave me some herbal pills and instructions for a detox. I know that I should give up wine, particularly white.

Whilst waiting for Alice, Mantak Chia walks down the corridor. I jump up and shake him by the hand and he welcomes me. I half expect him to look at me as if there is something special: I shrink back and don't tell him what I have been feeling. Why did I do that? What an idiot? What a missed opportunity! That's why I came to this place. Damn. It churns inside me, a huge regret which lasts for several days. I feel cross with myself. We fly on to Koh Samui for a week of beach. Way too busy for me but the kids enjoyed it.

22.08.11 Sent an email to James Oshman to tell him about my energy flow in the airport but he didn't reply. Maybe it's not that amazing after all.

30.08.11 Tennis at Fiona's. I forget to bring my glove and sleeve; I can't go back to get them because we don't have that much time today and I'll let the others down. I do my normal warm-up, pat ball in the service box, then play a set and a half of my normal tennis. No swelling, no soreness. That's the end of my glove and sleeve – I'll never put them on again! Wayhay!

07.09.11 Jamie is still around because he starts Leeds Uni in a couple of weeks. He shows me something on YouTube on his laptop, and carries it over to me as I am chopping carrots. The screen goes fuzzy; he says 'woah' and pulls it away. He tries again and has to pull it away again. 'Sorry, I think it's me.' He just looks at me and says, 'You're weird!'

24.09.11 Last weekend for the Living Anatomy course and I shall miss everybody. I pass with flying colours (87%) and I'm thrilled. If only I had done this earlier in my life – roll on the course proper.

29.09.11 My first practice client is Paula. I am not really sure what I am doing but I just lay my hands on various parts of her body, particularly her back, and she is thrilled. Says her back feels much better and books in for another in two weeks' time.

10.10.11 The Christmas fair season starts, and I decide that all my stationery stock must go. Prices slashed and hopefully I will have very little stock by Christmas, I have been carrying way too much. I'll carry on with the diaries because I have an enthusiastic following and they would be devastated if I stopped.

16.10.11 I go to Paula's again and give her a treatment. She is very receptive and has a good flow of energy. Don't know what I should be sensing but she is feeling better so that's all that matters.

19.10.11 – 23.10.11 The Biodynamic Craniosacral Therapy course starts! We sit in the usual bean bag or chair semi-circle. I look around at my fellow students and there isn't anyone I would make a beeline for to be my friend. I'll manage but they do seem an alien bunch. I have spent my life with the hunting, shooting, fishing crowd and I can honestly say I don't know a single vegetarian. This lot look like vegetarian tree huggers – not my scene at all.

Before we actually start, our tutor invites someone, anyone, to light the candle for the day. What?!

Sara, who is very keen, puts up her hand, goes over to the candle and gives a little speech. She says how blessed she is to be with such loving warm people and that it is an honour to light the candle on the first day of the first seminar. Oh my God, show me the door... If I hadn't already paid the first instalment, I would have been out of there like a shot.

There are all sorts of characters, all ages and several different nationalities. About seven have flown in from abroad. I befriend an Irish woman called Anna who is a dentist with her own practice. She is normal, very nice with a strong Irish accent so difficult to understand at times: she'll be my friend.

We have meditation sessions, hands-on practise and talks. It is fascinating stuff and yes, I can feel or sense lots of different types of energy. Just need to learn to put names to it and learn how to describe it to others so I know what it is that I am feeling. I can feel lots in my own body; more than I can feel in someone else's but if I can do that the rest is bound to come.

In one of our hands-on practice sessions on the treatment tables, Anna is the practice patient and someone else is doing the hands-on. I am also a practice patient on the next table with Paul as my practice practitioner. During the session, Anna shouts out and bangs the table with her legs. I have a little look at what is going on; her hands are 10 cm above her body, floating and she looks as if she is having a fit. I rest my head back down; weirdly, I don't find it at all scary and relax into the session. There's a commotion of tutors gathered around Anna's table, talking softly to her. Anna's wailing and banging goes on for several minutes, possibly eight or so, and then stops. At the end of the session, there is lots of crying from those who found the whole thing very disturbing. They stay on afterwards for hands-on from the tutors.

Anna looked as if she had seen God, if you could imagine what that might look like. She was all airy-fairy, cooing and her eyes were dazzlingly bright.

She said in her Irish drawl that she'd had 'a rocket up the arse' and that she had flown with birds and swam with fish. Oh, my goodness, that was my normal friend gone. She seems just as tree-huggingly odd as the rest of them now. Never mind, I'll just have to get on with it.

The next day Anna was still in La La Land with a grin on her face and a look as if to say, 'I've been there and you haven't.' She described it as a powerful surge from her sacrum which went right up her spine and out of her head. Then she was flying with birds and looking right into their eyes. She became a vegetarian in an instant!

By the end of the five days, the group felt like a whole unit and not fragmented individuals. I began to see them as lovely people despite their different backgrounds. I had a bit of a realisation: it really doesn't matter where you live or where you went to school or whether you are gay or straight or a meat eater or a vegetarian. After five days, these people had all become my friends and I'd lost the way I prejudge people before getting to know them. How refreshing that feels.

26.10.11 My sister Carey has mentioned to me several times about getting in touch with a chap called Dan Kahn. He is into Bi-Aura energy and used to be in the army with Angus, her husband. When somebody's name crops up more than once then I think of it as a message and that I should be doing something about it. So, I send Dan an email.

Dear Dan,
My sister, Carey Benson-Blair (wife of Bafi) has given me your details, not once but twice. I am now acting on them.

I was a normal, regular person who did not meditate nor even really understood the word holistic until recently! I was recovering from cancer and on 1st January 2011 (01.01.11 - amazing date) whilst reading a book about Reiki masters, I started feeling a strong buzzing in my body all over. It has been with me ever since. Sometimes very strong that it wakes me up in the night. I am sure that it has helped me to recover much quicker. I am now fully recovered and very healthy and the buzzing is still with me and getting stronger each day.

I have an incredibly sensitive body and can make certain organs move and even hear my SNS (sympathetic Nervous System) as a low buzz and can stop it! I have been doing healing on friends and family and seem to sort out back problems, frozen shoulders, tennis elbow and recently, a friend who although had a back problem cleared up arthritis in her hands; no more lumpy bits and she can pick up pans. All I do is put my hands on the body.

So having not done any biology I have recently completed a Living Anatomy course run by the Craniosacral Therapy Educational Trust and I have just started their practitioner training which takes 2 years. It is run as 4/5 day seminars every six weeks or so with practise in between.

But I listen to everyone with their feedback to hands-on practice sessions and I feel that no one has the feelings I have.

The energy buzz I am getting is really more of a body breathing (the CRI – cranial rhythmic impulse – in craniosacral terms) and I can feel the long tide without thinking about it. I can crash computers, check-out tills, dim lights and set off the hazard lights in the car. I am trying to calm this buzz down by focusing on my feet and when the build-up gets too much and I move my toes, it sounds like a crack of electricity. And this can happen often, perhaps once a minute, particularly at night.

I am enjoying the CST course but still feel that what I have is maybe more energy medicine. There are many more amazing things that have happened (including seeing people behind my eyes) but it would make the email too long for a first communication! I really hope you will reply and say, yes, I know exactly what you are feeling. No one has said that yet! I am not feeling very normal!

I look forward to your thoughts.

Regards,

Lulu

The reply comes back the same day.

Hi Lulu,

Yes! I know exactly what you are feeling! That's a relief, eh? I don't get the symptoms as strongly as you do but have experienced them on and off. It sounds like you have had a spontaneous Kundalini awakening and a very good one at that.

He then gives me a whole list of safety tips which I have listed at the end of the book. He also attaches an explanation of a Kundalini awakening and it is exactly what I have been experiencing.

We run a series of workshops to help people awaken their Kundalini and then what to do with it! We're about to rebrand so if you like I'll add you to my mailing list for the events I run and hopefully you'll be able to come along to one?

I hope that helps.

All the best,

Dan

'Hope that helps' – you bet it does. He knows what it is! I can't believe it! It's taken me ten months to get an answer. I am so grateful that I finally know.

A Kundalini awakening is a form of spiritual awakening, a connection with consciousness and there are two levels: the Lesser Kundalini awakening and the Greater. They can be induced but they can also be spontaneous. It can be frightening and sometimes painful and occasionally dangerous (none of these were my experience). It also affects individuals in different ways. It seems that what I have been going through in the past ten months is the Lesser one. And an extraordinary coincidence is that it seems Anna has had the Greater one. A spontaneous Greater awakening can be dangerous so I forward the email to my tutor, Tim, to let him know what it was that Anna had gone through so that they know how to deal with her situation (I am surprised that they obviously hadn't come across this).

27.10.11 Chris Evans on his Radio 2 Breakfast Show asks the question 'Why don't horses get jet lag when they travel to these big events in a plane and we humans do?'

I scream at the radio, 'Because they have metal shoes and ground themselves when they get off the plane.' Could write in but then they'll probably think I'm a bit strange so decide not to.

28.10.11 Mantak Chia comes to London to give a talk and I take a friend. We listen to his theories on female sexual energy and the Tao. All very interesting but I think the West is not ready for it. He talked of energies from the moon and mercury and it does seem to make sense. We are made up of nitrogen, phosphorus, iron, carbon, calcium, etc, with lots of water. About 75% of us is water, a similar percentage for the earth. So, if the Earth has a magnetic field and energy within and around it then it makes sense that we, too, have an energy in us.

24.11.11 I am back-to-back with selling my remaining stock at Christmas fairs and when I am not doing the fairs, I am at home sending off diary orders from the internet. It means long hours and is exhausting and leaves no time to do my homework. I try to do bits and pieces in between the fairs but I am running out of time.

Homework has to be in by 1st December, and I cannot get it done in time. I make the decision to tell my tutor, Tim, that I will have to be late with it. I am only allowed one 'late' homework throughout the whole course and I've managed to do it on my first one. I am so annoyed with myself because I secretly am very competitive so want to be the best in the group. Not a good start.

12.12.11 I finally get my homework done and emailed it.

15.12.11 I arrive on the first day of this second seminar and note that I feel like an individual and not part of the group. Bit by bit, we work out that everyone else feels the same. By the end of the day, we are all feeling united. We are cocooned in the building immersed in Craniosacral techniques and no one even mentions Christmas and it's only a week away. Anna is still a bit spaced out and when she is a practice patient she starts shaking again; the tutors think it is a trauma coming out. I had hoped they had read the email Tim circulated, but maybe not.

In our tutor groups, I ask Tim, 'Just a quick question...'

'No,' he stops me, 'slow down.' So, in a slow drawn-out voice, 'OK, one very slow question...' It seems that everyone is telling me to slow down. Except in my life outside this one, the old, normal one.

On the final day we, as a class, did a group 'tuning' into the long tide. The long tide is the energy around us; in CST-speak it is the Breath of Life which flows like a tide in and out, enveloping everything and everyone. It happens in 100-second cycles, 50 seconds coming in and 50 seconds going out. It was amazing, the room went cloudy and I felt as if I had dropped down a level but yet into a higher spiritual connection. Everywhere was fluid and had a motion to it. I left the seminar and walking down the street the world looked different. It was as if everyone was walking in a goldfish bowl. I'm finally getting the message. I'm not sure how many fellow students had the same feeling.

I arrive home and Richard is frustrated because I am so slow and not at all my usual chop-choppy self. It'll wear off, I reassure him.

But I am noticing that I have changed. Not only have I grown to appreciate people for what they are, by not judging them by their looks or caring about their backgrounds. The other big difference is that I realise that I want for nothing (other than perhaps to get married!). I used to have a mental list of things I desired or aimed for and probably felt a little disgruntled about not having them. That has gone. I am also feeling very humble; that an ego is not something to have. I am no better nor any more special than anyone else but I do know that I have a purpose in life and that I'm pursuing it.

26.12.11 The festive season begins. We have been to a family quiz, a champagne and shepherd's pie supper and countless drinks parties – right up the 'old me' street.

Christmas itself is at Frickley, the family home of Jayne and Charlie, my sister and brother-in-law. We are all there, Jamie included, 24 in all and we have such fun! A really ridiculous amount of presents. Richard, my brother-in-law, takes huge pleasure in wrapping up a naughty present from Ann Summers for each of the adults and puts on the label that they are from an Uncle Ronald! Funny thing was that Charlie actually has an Uncle Ronald and he couldn't understand why he would want to send him a black leather flogging whip!

Everyone in the family has different levels of intrigue on my new career path; the younger ones accept it completely, the older girls sort of accept it and the older men definitely don't accept it and positively shy away from it.

After Christmas lunch I had three practice patients, the younger ones of the family! My niece with a frozen shoulder, holding trauma from a fall from her pony, had a great benefit but she could do with another. I'm beginning to 'get it'.

31.12.11 Alice's friends come for New Year's Eve and we have a dinner party with games and one of them plays in the New Year with Auld Lang Syne on the bagpipes, then the games get a bit more racy and Richard and I bow out. It is a fab night, one of the best New Year's Eves.

09.01.12 As part of my course I have to practise the techniques learnt in the seminars. I am to do a minimum of two sessions a week. I have three willing friends who are happy to be regulars. I do all three today and give them each 50 minutes. We go to deep places of relaxation and I feel all sorts of rhythms. I can drop down and the room goes kind of foggy and sometimes I see waves of energy surrounding the body. Other times there seems to be energy dropping down into us like a radiator heat-haze, but falling towards us. I really keep focussing on my grounding because I don't want all this energy getting stuck in me.

11.01.12 January always means a lot of shooting for Richard and after a particularly good day we go to bed, and he snores. Not just little snores but raise-the-roof snores. So, in the dark, I decided to gently wake him up by putting a hand on his shoulder. Unbeknown to me he has his hand behind his head so instead of his shoulder, I get his armpit. He shoots up and sits bolt upright exclaiming, 'What?!! What's the matter?!!' But what was extraordinary was the reaction my body had. Adrenaline began racing through me. It was as if I had had the rude awakening. Goodness me, we almost seem to be one body. We certainly have our biospheres or auras crossing over each other.

As I lay there, getting over the shock of it, I thought of the starlings and how they fly so tightly together in stunning patterns of murmurations. They must be working as one with their biospheres merged into each other, otherwise it would be a shambles.

Another 'Oh, I get it moment', but surely others will be thinking along the same lines.

14.01.12 Richard is shooting again and I take the opportunity of going to London for an introductory course in the Bi-Aura technique that Dan Kahn is running. I really need to find out more about this world we live in; there's so much more to it.

As I listen to his lecture, he talks of the body's desire to return to health all the time. This is also the CST take on the body. He's quite an inspiration really. I recently have found dropping down a level extremely easy so I decide to try it whilst listening to him. I can see a white haze of energy around his head. I look at his assistant who is looking on from the side and can see a much bigger glow around her. Not colours, just white light.

He does a demonstration with one of the participants, she is standing and he holds his hands either side of her head pushing energy in towards her head. One hand is behind her head and the other is four feet in front. Slowly he moves the hand in front towards her brow. I can see the white energy between his hands! I am amazed! I discreetly tell him afterwards and he says that to see that is rare but not unknown.

25.01.12 Little op today to replace the breast implant that has gone hard after the radiotherapy and they do a 'Coleman fat transfer' from my tummy where they suck out fat cells and put them around the implant: this will make the finished item feel real. When I say little op, it was actually, three hours. I do my hands-on to myself and tune into the energy out in the universe. A week later, I was totally back to normal. Most people didn't even know I had had it. I have a week off healing others but go back to it the following week. It's all about listening to your body.

01.02.12 Lunch at the Fox and Hounds with my tennis four. One of them tells me, and this is the third time she's told me, to contact a friend of hers who is also a healer and lives about ten minutes away. Richard thinks of her as competition, but I think we need as many of us as possible. As Ralph says regarding my future clients, 'They'll come.'

I ring her the following day. She's called Nooky and we arrange to meet at our house the next morning at 9 a.m.

03.02.12 She is amazing, so alive and full of energy. Her eyes are dancing. We spend five hours together comparing our stories and techniques. She heals more in the Bi-Aura way of doing things. She has a mentor who trains her every so often and comes up from the south for a couple of days. A few days earlier she sent a despairing text to her mentor because she felt as if she was stagnating. Her text just said 'Help.' And then I rang her! I think we can support each other with these weird things going on that are happening to both of us. At least she won't think I'm bonkers!

09.02.12 I recognise now how much I have changed. I am a totally different person, no need to judge or label people, because I firmly believe that we are all just souls in bodies. Or are we bodies in souls? I feel whole, complete and above all, very happy.

12.02.12 The third seminar and I'm looking forward to getting together with my new-found friends. I found out that out of the 24 of us at least half are vegetarians. Wow, I now know a lot of vegetarians. We have a get-together with our tutors.

I've been feeling/sensing rhythms that don't make sense. Over these seminar days I learn of these rhythms, and I've been feeling them in advance of being taught. I thought I was just being bad at describing what I was feeling. I think the tutors presume that I couldn't be feeling that type of rhythm because we hadn't covered it on the course yet, so it was a relief as I am beginning to put all this together.

In one of the practice sessions, Patrick, a middle-aged full-of-life Frenchman was my 'practitioner.' I drop down into a deep state of relaxation (I learn during this seminar that this is referred to as The Holistic Shift; they teach us this but I've been doing it for weeks). I just feel deeply relaxed and safe.

When we finish the session Patrick retells his experience. He is amazed and says it is the most beautiful experience of his life. There are two white lights on either side of my pelvis. Out of one comes a beautiful butterfly which then flies about and lands on my left foot. It stays there a while flapping its wings and then it turns into a pool of gold which swirls around and then forms a gold bar connecting my feet.

He is so excited about this that he tells the whole class and he's still effusing about it several days later. I have no idea what it was or what it meant. I have no problems finding partners for the practice sessions after this episode! Fellow students seem keen to partner me and each one seems to say that they have just had a deep and special experience and they seem truly moved. I am on a high leaving.

14.02.12 I go for my regular session with Ralph and tell him briefly about some of my experiences. I ask him, and this is the first time I have specifically asked, to ask my or his guides if there are any messages. There are lots!

- They are impressed with how I have coped and recovered from my illness both physically and emotionally.
- They are pleased with how my training is going
- I should be more open and question more

He then said, 'Oh, goodness, they have asked me to facilitate the opening of the third eye.' So, he circled his finger between my eyebrows and then moved his finger from the centre of this spot in outward motions. This lasted about 20 seconds and then his fingers became moistened. He said it was naturally produced healing balm.

The session ended and he said, 'That doesn't happen often,' and I gave him a hug.

I left his house and noticed my field of vision was wider and seemed to be able to see around the sides of me as well as in front. Definitely a big difference. I will check what the third eye is on the internet later.

18.02.12 Went to CC's house, one of my regular practice patients, and she was telling everyone how she hadn't been pain-free for many years. She looks younger and with a less pained, stress-free expression on her face. I played it down because half of me thinks wow, I must be good, and the other half is very uncomfortable with that feeling. I am the channel and it's not me doing anything. I'll try and keep that thought and keep my ego out of it.

29.02.12 As part of my training, I have to receive a course of treatments from a Biodynamic CST practitioner. Well, there aren't any around the East Midlands area. I have had a couple of treatments from someone in Stamford who is very good but not biodynamic. So I go to visit Lenka who did the same course four years ago. She lives in London and has a room in a yoga centre in Putney. I am amazed she can do work in a room without a window. I certainly couldn't.

What she came up with was strange. She said my right pelvic area was energetically dead. She said that the top half of my body was open and beautiful but the bottom half was dark and inert as if my body was two different bodies. She hadn't experienced this before. She worked on getting my pelvis going but said it would take time. She said it felt like old, deep-seated fear.

Mmm, that's weird, I don't know what that was all about.

01.03.12 I email Lenka.

Hi Lenka,

Thank you for the treatment. I am having thoughts that maybe the deep-seated fear may be from another life. I don't think I am going bonkers, but I keep having thoughts about knife wounds and also thoughts about appendicitis. Will see if there is anything that comes from my spiritual healer.

Regards,

Lulu

I've never really thought about past lives but it suddenly popped into my head that it could be a possibility. Maybe we get more than one go at things; some religions, like Buddhism, believe in karma and that past lives really is a thing.

02.03.12 Mary from the village is recovering from breast cancer and she comes for a treatment. I am supposed to be healing healthy people but felt that I couldn't refuse particularly when I know what she is going through.

I carry out the session in the spare bedroom. We are fortunate, or our guests are, to have an en-suite bathroom off it. The bathroom has no windows and during this session the door was slightly ajar.

I began at her feet, with my hands gently resting on them, and then moved to the sacrum with my hand at the base of her spine and then onto the head, my hands underneath cupping it.

I noticed a white glow in the bathroom. It was about 4 feet high and in the gap of the door and its surround. There is no window in there. I felt as if there was someone there. I thought that I would acknowledge this 'thing' and I smiled, letting it know that I was aware of its presence. It then came into the room and stayed at Mary's feet. It got wider and seemed to split but maybe there were two of them. They stayed there until the end of the session.

I didn't tell Mary; I think she may have run away and never come back. I didn't tell Richard either. But I felt truly blessed and whole.

08.03.12 Ralph again. I tell him about my sighting of a spirit and he just smiles a knowing smile. It's good to be able to talk to someone about it. Nooky is too busy with small children at the moment so haven't met up with her again, but it'll happen.

I ask Ralph, 'OK, a bit of a tall order but one of my tutors told me I had an old soul and I wondered if I had had previous lives? And have any of them been traumatic?'

He closed his eyes with his hands hovering around my head and told me immediately that about five lives ago I had a particularly horrible death. I was buried alive in the sand and tortured to death. I was a man and it happened in Sudan. My hands were bound and weighted down and I was left in the sun to die and for the birds and animals to feed on.

What?! Oh, my goodness, this is truly wacky stuff! But I felt grief, tears rolled down my cheeks and into my ears. I couldn't stop them.

He again reiterated to be aware of who I meet because I wear my heart on my sleeve and some are not what they seem. He rubs the sides of my temples as he says the words.

He also tells me another message from above, that I will soon see colours from my hands as I heal people.

At the end of the session, I double-checked the past life story, scrutinising Ralph's eyes as he speaks; he looks genuine, he believes this, he's not making it up.

When I get home, I email Lenka. I cannot possibly tell anyone else this. This confirms to me that we are souls in bodies and I used to be a black man living in Sudan! I could never 'prove' that it really happened. Why didn't I dig myself out? Maybe I was buried from the neck down? After some searching online, it is called immurement and it did exist where the victims were left to die from starvation or dehydration. All I can say is that it really resonated with me, it felt true, an inner knowing. I certainly grieved today for it. Wow, I am a white woman now and I used to be a black man in a previous life – wow!

Richard said the other day, 'All I wanted was a normal girlfriend.' If I told him this, he really would think I'd gone bonkers.

09.03.12 I have been practising on willing friends whenever I can. I go to Essex, my old stomping ground, at two weekly intervals and do six in a day. I put Mondays aside for them and do local clients on the other alternate Mondays. Each time I practise, wonderful things happen. Sometimes they feel it and sometimes they are blissfully unaware. I do not tell them of spirits being present: except for Helen, who is spiritually aware and felt a presence for herself.

When I am in a practice session and more likely at home rather than in other people's homes, I get a sense of a white light, usually about 4 feet by 2 feet and it moves. One time from another room, other times it is on top of the wardrobe but they quite often come closer. Ralph once told me that sometimes the spirits come and visit to learn from what we are doing! I found that more than a little disappointing – I would have expected them to be all-knowing. Around half my sessions are involving the spirits – I do feel blessed.

However, I am finding that quite often the client leaves feeling great and I end up with their ailment. Anything from stress, sadness to back problems or headaches. I must work out how to stop this happening. Not good for my own health.

There has been another strange phenomenon and it has happened four times so far and becoming more amazing each time it happens. When we are deeply relaxed and in CST-speak, in touch with the universal energy of the long tide, waves of colours come down from the ceiling in wing-like motions – big blobs of purple and green. It descends down and into the patient and is a very other-worldly connection, like the aurora borealis. Deep healing seems to happen when in this state. We call it dynamic stillness.

Something has been worrying me though. Where they replaced the implant, in the area of the skin being very thin as a result of the radiotherapy, I notice a tiny hole along the scar line. A good holiday and lots of rest will help it to knit together, I'm sure. We have booked a last minute, cheap, ten days in Sharm El-Sheikh.

22.03.12 In Egypt and been thinking about the colours descending from above during sessions. Maybe that was what Ralph was talking about. Maybe he got the message from guides that I would be able to see colours and he wrongly interpreted and added something himself by saying that the colours would come from my hands. Will ask him on my next visit.

I have a lovely holiday being normal with Richard but I'm a little concerned that I am being watched during sex. So, before anything happens, I ask them not to look! Does it mean that they have been watching me all of my life, what a thought! Uncomfortable feeling but quite amusing!

11.04.12 Had a phone call from my sister, Daphne, who reported that Uncle Donald, who is in a hospice, has only a few days to go. I go up to Yorkshire to visit. He doesn't seem that bad and I'm sure he has longer than that. I had an overwhelming desire to tell him I loved him, for the first time ever and I reassured him that there is life beyond this world and not to be frightened. He wasn't convinced! I said that when he gets there he can look down and I'll be saying, 'I told you so.'

Feeling wracked with guilt for not offering to do some hands-on but he has cancer all over his body and I am struggling with my boundaries and grounding and I just daren't do it.

19.04.12 Day one of the fourth seminar. I really get what they are saying but there are some things that happen that are over and above the CST concept. I told Tim, my tutor, of a regular practice patient, who is normally so open and easy to read. The last time she came her body was full of anxiety and stress. It showed me nothing but blind panic. I couldn't feel any flows at all. So, I said in my head, and addressing her body, to let it go. The energy flowed from her and into me. Wow! Big grounding taking place. This lasted about 30 seconds and then I began to feel the other flows I was looking for. She felt an emptying of stress too.

Also, what I am interpreting as the long tide with the colours descending, is, I think, a spiritual phenomenon. I feel a bit alienated in the class because I feel that these extra bits don't seem to be happening to others. Or maybe they are keeping quiet too! Will try and discuss with Tim about grounding and protecting myself.

20.04.12 I didn't discuss with Tim but did talk to Annabel. Actually, it is the first time I have ever had a conversation with her. She said she grounds herself morning and night by imagining a bubble around her and then a cloak over the top.

She explained her technique so that's what I thought I would have as part of my daily routine from now on. I think I am too open due to the Kundalini awakening. Others don't seem to have as big a problem with grounding. She also sees auras/colours around people and had a spiritual guide! So, there are others on the course like me! What a relief!

23.04.12 I do my new morning ritual of putting myself in a bubble and then wrapping a cloak around me. I feel more contained, it's extraordinary. Let's hope it protects me without restricting my connection to above. Little hole in the skin is still there, so I book an appointment with the consultant.

24.04.12 Go in to get the hole stitched up. I am awake and in theatre. No anaesthetic or pain relief because it's numb anyway! We chat away throughout it. In and out of the hospital in under three hours – must be a record.

25.04.12 I visit Uncle Donald for what I know will be the last time. He just lies in bed with laboured breathing and is unaware of my arrival. I put my right hand under his shoulders and my left in his left hand. I cannot feel any flows or rhythms. After a few minutes his erratic breathing settles and he becomes more settled – the whole room seems to settle too.

I stay for a couple of hours and he is at peace. Not totally convinced I had anything to do with it but maybe. I still feel guilty about not doing something at my previous visit.

Lying in bed that night, I feel a pressure spot under and to the right of my implant. As we spent a lot of time in the last seminar on 'augmenting fulcrums' – that is initiating energy into blocked energy, a bit like smashing a boulder in a river so the river can flow freely – I thought I'd try to release the fulcrum I was feeling under my right boob. Why not practise on myself? I release it and get a strong glow of heat down my right side towards the base of my spine and up my back and right up to the top of my head. Wow, it was a wonderful feeling. I listen again to that area, the pressure point (it felt as if someone had their thumb pressing inside me) had gone but there was another fulcrum further left towards the midline. my spine. I released that too and then there was another and we continued for many more. Now this is a real lesson, multiple fulcrums in traumatised areas.

I think this is work in progress and not a quick fix because there's more to be done, but it has been a great way to practise the techniques taught in the last seminar.

27.04.12 Uncle Donald died at 5.20 a.m. I was in bed at home and awake in deep meditation. I felt as if I was really connecting and I asked them to help. By 'them' I think I mean my spiritual guides, my team of helpers. It felt like they were trying to get in touch and I was trying to speak but I just couldn't work out how. I am still a novice at this game.

During the course of the morning, several times, I looked up to the skies and said, 'I told you so.'

28.04.12 The first thing we do in the morning is open the curtains and shut the window. Whilst getting dressed I notice a puff of wind and ask Richard, 'What was that? Is the window open?' 'No.' comes the reply.

I notice it again but coming from the other direction. I can't see anything. Perhaps it is a visitation – perhaps it is Uncle Donald.

03.05.12 I still feel as if my body is not happy and am putting it down to emotion. Helping my sister with the funeral arrangements has been emotionally exhausting and a real reminder of my father's death in 1994.

I text Nooky to see if she can give me a treatment. Would be interesting to find out how she does her healing anyway.

I get there at noon and go to her room above the garage. There is a very strong energetic feeling about it. We have a chat first and then we begin. I sit on a chair in the middle of the room with my hands on my legs and I close my eyes. She does lots of swirling with her hands a few inches from my body and she concentrates on the chakras. At the heart chakra we both get a real sense of needing to get rid of something and my body not wanting to let go. It was a weird tug-of-war feeling with my energy. I felt lots of tingling all over but particularly up my left side.

We both agree that it was a great session and we decide that at some stage I will need to get rid of this emotional baggage that is hanging over me.

04.05.12 I have the stitches taken out and it is still not quite knitting together so they put steri-strips on it and a dressing and will check it in a week. My breast skin is very thin and with the radiotherapy damaging it, the skin cells are struggling to join.

In hindsight, the radiotherapy was an unnecessary measure. Having chopped the whole boob off and chemotherapy and taking tamoxifen every day, I think that would have been enough. We only have one body and it's up to us to look after it. Goodness knows why cancer rates are so high in the West, but my theory is a combination of things and there's no scientific proof.

Firstly, when it comes to lifestyle – we live a stressful life, rushing about, on-call all day and night because of telephones. We never switch off and listen to our bodies in order to allow them to heal themselves. That's what I have discovered CST to be all about: the body has an inherent treatment plan and will do its own healing in the order it wants to do it. And we don't take time out and allow it to do this. In the Far East, they do, with meditation and their cancer rates are much lower.

When it comes to diet, I do think we eat too much dairy. The amount of oestrogen in cow's milk is very high because it has to make a calf grow quickly. We do not need so much oestrogen. The East eats very few dairy products; they eat lots of fresh fruit and vegetables – freshly cooked. Sugar too, way too much in our diets. Alcohol, also, and ultra-processed foods. It's just not doing us any good.

The other thing is that since the invention of the pill, the oestrogen levels in water have been increasing and they haven't worked out a way of extracting it yet. The head of the Trout and Salmon Association told me that it's affecting fish.

05.05.12 May Bank Holiday and a weekend away with the children in a friend's holiday cottage in Shropshire. I love it when we are all together in my recently formed family. We all get on so well and have such fun together.

We go on a big walk up The Mynd and look over to Wales in the west and England in the east. We walk along it and then down through a wood. It is a lovely walk but I am exhausted and lag behind. Maybe it is because of the chemotherapy – I will never be able to do what I did before in the way of exercise. I also come down with a real stinker of a cold, the first ailment in 18 months.

I have a pain under my implant, I wonder if it is my body rejecting it. It's like a muscle spasm and I think there's a big fulcrum there. It feels similar to when I had a drain in and my tissues went into spasm and tried to reject it. I send a text to Nooky saying that I think it is not emotion but the implant itself. My body doesn't want it and I can't get rid of it.

08.05.12 What a day! We all get ready for the funeral: Mummy, the sisters and other halves and children, fifteen of us in all, meet up for lunch beforehand. I am feeling stressed and my sister, Jayne, notices. It goes well, if a funeral can go well. I do a reading and just manage to hold it together.

I'm Free by Anne Lindgren Davison

Don't grieve for me for now I'm free.
I'm following the path God laid for me.
I took his hand when I heard him call.
I turned my back and left it all.

I could not stay another day,
To laugh, to love, to work, or play.
Tasks left undone must stay that way,
I've found that peace at the close of day.

If my parting has left a void,
Then fill it with remembered joy.
A friendship shared, a laugh, a kiss,
Ah yes, these things I too will miss.

Be not burdened with times of sorrow:
I wish you the sunshine of tomorrow.
My life's been full I've savoured much,
Good times, good friends, a loved one's touch.

Perhaps my time seemed all too brief,
Don't lengthen it now with undue grief.
Lift up your heart and share with me,
God wanted me now, he set me free.

It seemed so appropriate. About 150 people turn up to the funeral with standing room only. Not bad for someone who is 82; it just shows what a popular man he was. He would have enjoyed it.

11.05.12 At the hospital they take off the dressing and steri-strips. It hasn't worked, there is still a little hole. The skin just won't knit together. Another blow. What happens next? The consultant is not on duty that day so I arrange to pop back on Monday.

13.05.12 I have a busy weekend and by Sunday night I am exhausted. Tomorrow, I go to Yorkshire to spend a few days sorting out Uncle Donald's house and have arranged lots of appointments with estate agents, valuers and house clearance companies.

14.05.12 Monday morning and I feel sick. I throw up before even getting dressed. Something's wrong. I look in the mirror and my right boob is very red. Bugger. This looks like an infection. This is not good news.

I stay in bed and put my hands on my hips and tune into my body's rhythms. My central nervous system is very agitated and my body is under stress. It feels the same as one of the practice client's body did – definitely under stress.

The consultant rings me to arrange a time to meet. Richard takes me at 12. They want to admit me for intravenous antibiotics but instead give me some very strong pills, the type they give for MRSA. I nervously ask if it is

MRSA, no is the answer. Phew. I cancel all arrangements I had made in Yorkshire; health comes first.

17.05.12 Over the past two days I have visited three different consultants. One of the consultants who is based at the Marsden in London is the one I choose to go with and trust him implicitly. We discuss where I will stay after the op and I mention my lifelong friend Mancy, in Putney and it turns out he lives next door to her. That is more than extraordinary. That shows I have definitely chosen the right person.

I decide to have a reconstruction using my tummy. My body is not happy having a foreign body in it and I just can't go to flat and have no breast at all. So, the plan is to have the op on the 16th July and take the summer to recover. I have Olympic final tickets for the rowing 8s on the 1st August so I'll have to give them to someone else.

At least there'll be lots of sport to watch on the TV whilst recovering. And I won't feel guilty watching daytime TV. Always turn something negative into a positive – that's my motto!

25.05.12 I receive an email from my new consultant who says he is not happy about leaving it until July and is bringing it forward to 18th June.

This is a few days before my course's residential seminar at a retreat in Herefordshire. This is a huge disappointment. I have to be sensible and cancel it. I talk to my new tutor, Tracy, and she understands and is very sympathetic. I also tell her about my uncle's death. She is amazed at how calm I am!

My uncle's house can wait so there's no point stressing about that. The water's been turned off so not much can go wrong, and the wonderful neighbours are keeping an eye on the place.

My main priority is me. I have to look after my body. What I hadn't realised was that once you have an infection in something like an implant, it is impossible to kill. It is possible to treat an infection in tissue with antibiotics but not an infection in a foreign body so I am on double dose antibiotics which is keeping the infection at bay. I go to bed for a couple of hours, meditate and tune in and give my body some time and attention. It has to be well enough to fight this infection and I need the skin to be as healthy as possible.

I cancel all my practice patients' appointments. My next seminar is cancelled and so I now put my spiritual journey on hold and concentrate on getting better. This must have been building up over several weeks. My healing with Nooky, my tiredness, my cold, it all makes sense. I have been fighting this infection for a while and with all the other stresses going on, it has started to win.

There's something bigger going on

2. FREEDOM

At any moment, you have a choice, that either leads you closer to your spirit or further away from it. Letting go gives us freedom and freedom is the only condition for happiness. If, in our heart, we still cling to anything – anger, anxiety or possessions – we cannot be free
– Thick Nhat Hanh

G ot the diary sent down from Leicestershire – there's just so much going on, I must get it down on paper. I was thinking that I would have some time off writing it. There's more than ever happening now. Have to recap over the past few days...

04.06.12 So to recap, last Wednesday I went to my local hospital to get the dressing changed. I am on strong antibiotics, trying to keep everything at bay. The nurse called for the consultant to take a look. They weren't happy with it ... they weren't?... I wasn't! I suggested that we should ditch the dressings and let some good old-fashioned fresh air to it. I take a photo with my phone and feeling a little panicky as if the situation is getting out of control, I send it to my London consultant with Help! Urgent! in the subject line. I told him that I didn't like the look of it, that it felt as if my skin is rotting away and that my local consultant suggest she would operate on Friday and swap it to a temporary expandable implant.

He replied within the hour *'This needs dealing with sooner rather than later and no don't do the temporary option. My secretary will be in touch with you.' Sent from my iphone.*

I'm impressed.

Half an hour later his secretary rings, I am to get to the Marsden for 2 pm tomorrow when I shall be admitted and then operated on this Saturday if he can get a team together because it's the Queen's Golden Jubilee Bank Holiday weekend and the whole country is on holiday.

We head south, and on the way, I ring Ralph to cancel my appointment for tomorrow. 'They'll be looking after you, it's coming through very strongly, so don't worry.' I tell Richard this and he says that he bets he says that to everyone. I don't think so but keep quiet. That's enough for Richard in one conversation.

So, we arrive and get shown into a lovely room, double aspect as they say in estate agent speak; one across the Fulham Road and the other down it. It's good to get the plan underway and I feel in safe hands.

Richard leaves, a good thing, because he can't cope with hospitals and he's got that 'Oh my god, she's going to die look on his face' and I don't want an attitude like that!

They send me off for a CT scan to check for the state of the blood vessels after my Coleman fat transfer in January and I really hope they haven't been damaged.

I get hooked up for intravenous antibiotics. Digby arrives with some oranges because they are good for my immune system and Alice calls in too – it's on her bus route. It is good to see them.

I feel confident that I am on the right path. All is well now.

The next morning, Friday, my consultant pops in and tells me that the blood vessels don't look badly damaged. 'Thank goodness for that, what I relief.' I said.

'But...' – I didn't like the sound of that – 'We have discovered a mark on your liver which needs further investigation.' He tried to reassure me with, 'It's more than likely nothing because lots of us wander around with blemishes like that.' My head was spinning. No! This is not supposed to happen! This is not part of the big plan! I am not going to deliver this news to Richard.

Mancy, my friend from Putney and the consultant's neighbour, calls in and decides she is going to stay for a while. She calms and reassures me. But there is so much going on with nurses and doctors, so she leaves.

I spend the afternoon sorting out getting a cannula in blood vessels that have been damaged by chemo, seven attempts in all, having a 'before' photo (it's looking pretty yucky so I insist on no head in the photo!) and having an ultrasound. The doctor carrying out the ultrasound tells me the good news, that it is a blemish that is benign as it is light coloured. Panic over.

I send Mancy a text: 'Phew.'

Richard, looking very uncomfortable pops in that evening with Jamie, and they can't wait to get out! I find it quite funny!

Saturday 2nd June is operation day and I get up early at 5.30 a.m. and shower. The boob is looking pretty bad now where the skin has gone black and broken down. I really hope they find enough good tissue to attach the tummy to. I definitely couldn't do another day.

The TV is on as a background noise and distraction. The nurse comes in at about 6 p.m. and is surprised I am up and about. She gives me a gown to put on and compression thigh-length stockings.

6.45 a.m. and there's a knock on the door. It's Mancy! She couldn't bear to think that I was on my own before such a big operation. I have to admit that the emotional pressure was beginning to build up in me so having Mancy to talk to and being a bigger distraction than the Golden Jubilee on the TV, was fantastic.

Then her neighbour, also known as my consultant, Paul, pops in to discuss what's going to happen with the op. I told him that he should look on me as he would his wife and if anything cropped up that was difficult just do what he would do to his own wife. I could ask no more.

I walk down to theatre, waving goodbye to Mancy. What a good friend.

I am in the outer bit of the theatre and about to be put to sleep and notice the time – 7.40 a.m.

I am being woken up and I look at the clock, can't remember what the time said but it was around the same time as when I last looked.

'Oh, no, you haven't been able to do it.' A flash of panic went through my head, and 'What now?' I thought.

They reassured me that it had been done and that it was now early evening. Wow, it must have been a long operation.

I go into intensive care which is a room with four beds each divided by drawn curtains. I was attached to several beeping machines, a catheter and four drains – I've looked better! Alice comes to visit and she looks at me with eyes welling up. 'Don't you dare,' I tell her. I couldn't cope with a crying daughter.

So, my night of torture begins. Not only beeping machines but blood pressure being automatically tested and a Doppler, which looks like a pen, was used every hour to check that the blood vessels attached in my new boob were behaving themselves. They made the most wonderfully happy sounds – it sounded like "Wow, wow, wow" about every second which made me think that the whole area was very happy. So, in between all my tests and bleeping, my ICU neighbours were also being tested and bleeped at. Absolutely impossible to sleep. Boy, I was tired.

Sunday 3rd June and they push me in my bed back to my room on the third floor. I feel as if I have been run over by a bus. Not pain because I had drugs to stop that, but I felt totally traumatised.

Richard and Jamie call in looking smart for their Fishmongers lunch and seats overlooking the Jubilee River Pageant. They looked shocked at seeing me. Some of the doctors who had worked on me came to check me over and details emerged: the operation was ten hours, the team was nine with three of them being the surgeons. They said the scar tissue around the implant was the most they had ever seen. I also had low haemoglobin and low potassium.

I thanked them all profusely for giving up their Bank Holiday Saturday. Richard and Jamie did a sharp exit, Richard's face was drained of blood and needed some fresh air!

Throughout that day, my hands felt extremely buzzy as if there was masses of energy coming from them. I held the cot sides of the bed trying to keep my hands away from my body. It felt too soon, my body was too traumatised to have any healing, it was just too, too sore. Occasionally, my hands would rest on my body and I could feel hot and burning inside. I turned my palms out so that any energy was radiating out and away from me. I began to get a bit exasperated with my healing hands so shouted out loud 'No! Stop! It's too soon!' and in an instant, the energy stopped from my hands and they felt totally normal.

Now that was interesting. A couple of times during the day, my hands started buzzing again and I just talked to them and said, no, not yet. It was amazing, they responded.

I asked for the nurses to do everything at the same time because I so needed my sleep. Please could they do blood pressure, pill giving, Doppler blood vessel testing all at the same time not individually? I cried because I was so very, very tired.

The river pageant looked spectacular what glimpses I saw on my little TV on an arm, but I didn't care.

Back to today. They get me up and I sit on a chair having transported drains and catheter with me – it is really exhausting. I have a tiny breakfast and then back to bed.

They take out the catheter.

I lie in my bed just gazing out of the window. Then begins an energetic sensation that seems to be coming from out there in the universe. It gives me an all-over buzz, much more intense than my usual buzz, there are wave-like motions too, not only in my body but around it too. This could be the long tide. It felt as if it had to 'do its stuff' and my body was having a gentle treatment and it wanted to do its own thing.

So, I decided to give in and said out loud 'Go on then but please be gentle.'

It felt as if I was plugged into a recharger. A lovely, gentle wave-like motion not only all over and around but within. A kneading feeling as if being massaged from inside. Other times it felt as if I had a laser inside knitting it all together, with lines being etched inside my left abdomen, going back and forward. It really was a fantastic feeling, very humbling because this was happening all on its own. I didn't feel as if my body was doing it, it felt as if there was something else directing it. It lasts for hours.

I rang Ralph and told him. He knowingly acknowledged everything I told him. This was very exciting.

I watch the Jubilee concert that evening and I go to the loo and come back dancing to Madness with four drips tubes in my right hand – the nurse comes in and we both have a good laugh. I hear the fireworks through the window. A fitting end to my day too!

05.06.12 This buzzing, flowing, kneading and laser stitching doesn't switch off. It is with me all day and all night. It crescendos with intermittent intensity and I'm loving it.

The consultant pops in and says he is happy with everything except the haemoglobin count which because of the loss of blood and replacing with fluids I haven't enough red blood cells carrying nutrients around my body. If the blood count doesn't start going up by tomorrow I'll need a blood transfusion. I felt sure that I wouldn't need one, my body was sorting itself out.

First drip is taken out.

I ring Lou, my old friend whose house we stayed in Mauritius and tell her about the healing that is going on. Whilst I am telling her, I notice an energetic distortion, like a pixel distortion on the TV; it's quite large, probably 6 feet by 4 feet and up in the air to my right-hand side. Nothing on the left. The phone line gets distorted too, and Lou can't hear me. 'I'm losing you,' she says. I said 'There's some funny energetic distortion going on, it's weird. I'll ring you back.'

It momentarily subsides and I redial her number. After a few moments, it happens again. It looks like a mixture of when the pixels get distorted on the television with a slightly metallic look and a heat haze. 'The phone's going funny again,' she says. 'Oh, I've got that funny energy stuff going on again, I'll ring you back later,' and with that, we lost connection.

I look to my right and say out loud, 'OK then, I give in, do what you have to do.' I receive the most wonderfully powerful energetic kneading, an internal massage as if I am being recharged. Not just inside my body but all around. In fact, I wasn't aware of an end to my body. I existed in a sea with no end or beginning. It was very intense and lasted fifteen minutes.

I ring Ralph to tell him and to ask if he had just been working on me remotely. He said no but that I was being worked on by my guides all the time. I said, 'Too right, they don't leave me alone!' As I say goodbye, I am about to disconnect the phone, I hear Ralph say, 'Enjoy the journey.'

I group-text a list of wacky friends and ask them whether they had been working on me. They all had at some stage sent healing vibes, but not at the precise time. This takes me most of the afternoon. I thought I could have proved something because I knew the exact time, 12.15 to 12.30, but no one has been transmitting (tongue in cheek!) at that time.

I am finding it all quite amusing and challenging. I look for reasons and try to understand why. I thought maybe when it began on Monday it had something to do with the morphine I was on, but I'm off it now and the only pills I am taking is paracetamol and diclophenac. I've had those pills before and never felt anything like this before.

06.06.12 Had some great healing last night; very intense and really felt as if my body was being worked on and stroked and gently manipulated in a very precise way. I could even feel right inside my bones tingling, the bone marrow maybe.

Haemoglobin is up today, so no blood transfusion. Good, I think my body has been through enough already.

Two more drips come out, only one more to go.

Anna comes to visit. She looks smug when I tell her of what's been going on, not only the healing but the distortions when I was on the phone. She keeps the same smug look and has a few cryptic sentences, which I just do not understand. She's definitely away with the fairies. I text her later to thank her for coming and she says that there were others in the room and that angels were looking after me.

Helen and Nicky also come to visit and as they are quite in tune with their spiritual side, I tell them too about what has been going on. They are fascinated.

I have to be careful who I tell because the majority of people just don't 'get it.' Not sure how much I actually 'get' but I am learning fast.

Richard, for instance, would run a mile if he knew the half of what's been going on. I absolutely hate keeping things from him because I have always been a firm believer in that you should have a very open relationship and be truthful about everything. He'd run away if he knew. I will drip-feed him bits when I think he's being receptive. Sometimes he glazes over or looks a bit frightened, so that's the time to stop and save it for another day.

I am still feeling the warm, energetic flow in and around me. Every so often, I have several minutes of the laser treatment or some pulling and pushing inside me. Earlier today, my left forearm was tingling between the wrist and the elbow. I have had eight different cannulas and many tens of needles in order to get them in. They finally ended up putting it in my foot instead. My veins kept disintegrating when they put in the antibiotics. Maybe the arm tingling was my veins being attended to.

07.06.12 Last night, there was some incredible healing that intensified so much it woke me up; I gasped and shouted out. I was dripping with sweat but not hot. My body certainly was getting rid of something, perhaps the anaesthetic? This happened about three times.

The last drip is taken out today. I'm getting good at breathing out when they pull it out, so it doesn't hurt. A real relief not to be attached to anything when I walk about. I'm not a great handbag carrier at the best of times. They tell me I can go home tomorrow. I need to define 'home.' Having prewarned Mancy about staying with her I now confirm it by text. It is particularly convenient having the consultant living next door in case I need him. The answer is yes, but she can't pick me up. Mummy and my sister, Daphne, come and visit all the way from Yorkshire – a sterling effort. They are both amazed at how well I look; I don't let on at all about the wacky stuff that's been going on. Mummy takes a photo and then one of Daphne and compares the two – the verdict is that I look fitter than my sister – ha! Thank you, up there!

08.06.12 The healing just continues but again was fairly intense whilst I slept, crescendoing like the night before, twice. It has a cleansing feel about it. The buzzing and kneading still goes on during the day. I really feel as if I am being looked after.

Release date is today. I can't wait for freedom, but also feel a little nervous. Paul, my consultant, comes to say goodbye and promises to knock on the door occasionally to see how I am. He's also happy for me to knock on his door if I have any concerns. I love the synchronicity of this!

Sara, the one who lit the candle, comes to visit and offers to take me to Mancy's in Putney for my two-week recuperation, saving a taxi. She brings a huge bunch of flowers from everyone on the course. How kind they are. She also gives me a blessings card, a gold card, a bit like a credit card but made of metal. It is supposed to protect… I think I'm doomed to be wacky now!

I've got an end-of-term feeling and have become a bit institutionalised, so getting outside and the world getting bigger as I go feels a bit weird. I now know what being released from prison must feel like, and my sentence wasn't very long. We find the key, Sara helps me with my case and we head for my bedroom. I'm so grateful to Sara.

My bedroom has a four-poster bed in it and is on the first floor but the bathroom is on the ground floor, and worse still, the kitchen and sitting room are in the basement. This all feels such a challenge, and it's hard work just doing a few steps.

During the daytime, both Mancy and her husband, Steven, are at work. My bedroom has a lovely view of a tree with parrakeets flying in and out of it all day long. Mancy leaves food for me in my room but the desire to go to the sitting room to watch TV is zero, mainly because I'll have to climb the stairs to get back to my room. I know my strength will improve, but with time. So, with no TV, no radio and no inclination to read a book, I stay in my room and remain quiet, sometimes asleep and sometimes awake. All the time, my body is busy, busy repairing itself. It's good that there's nothing to distract me; maybe it is supposed to happen like this. I do need quiet time.

Mancy had researched food that is good for raising the haemoglobin, so I get delicious beetroot-based delicacies and red wee.

10.06.12 Richard popped in yesterday and stayed for an hour. Other than that, I have had no visitors whilst staying in my town house – perfect. This allows me time to recharge my batteries. There aren't many people who come and visit and leave me full of energy. Most leave me drained, so no visitors is a blessing. So, my days are spent healing and eating very healthy food.

I mull over the conversations with Anna and go through my messages on my phone. I text her again and tell her I don't feel alone. She replied suggesting, 'Just try to talk to them.'

At a time when there was no one in the house, I thought I'd give it a go. It began with 'OK, I know I'm not mad, but...' There was nothing in response, no gut feeling, nothing popping in my head. But then my brain was very active. I felt as if it was in control of what I was trying to do. So, I lay there and tried in vain to switch off my brain.

I then try a brain-clearing technique someone had told me about. Count slowly to ten and make sure the brain does not come up with something. If it does, start again at one. I couldn't get past three, so I gave up.

I continued the following day with the brain-clearing technique and trying to communicate with my guides. I have no idea what I am doing or whether it was the right way to do it. I did it silently, waiting for another picture maybe, or a word to pop into my head, but I am still finding it difficult to clear the brain.

15.06.12 I tried a different tack today. I let myself go really relaxed, into the deep space of dynamic stillness. My body is alive, like every cell is buzzing. I don't know what to say and to whom. So, I start with thanking them for everything they have done for me. I then asked them to show me a sign for a 'yes' so that I could ask them questions. Maybe I would hear, see or feel something, but what I did get a sense of was a pulling down in the middle of my head. It was very gentle and just off-centre to the right, almost behind my eye. I then asked, 'Show me a 'no' and I get a pulling up, from the same area, up towards the top of my head.

Wow, this is exciting; I ask lots of questions so that I could learn to interpret it when feeling these sensations. So, this is the start of my communication and I spend the next few hours asking questions and getting replies. I just kept practising.

'Should I carry on seeing Ralph?' Pull down: yes.

'Should I become a healer?' Pull down, yes.

'Should I carry on writing my journal?' Pull down, yes.

'Should I go on TV?' Pull up, no.

'Should we sell Uncle Donald's house?' Pull down, yes.

Wow, I was amazed. I didn't seem to be imagining it. I was so excited about it and had no one to tell.

In the middle of the night, I woke and slowly glanced around the room through half-opened eyes. I noticed on the left of the ceiling a glow of light. It didn't move or change in size, but remained there. I tried to work out whether it was a reflection of the moon, maybe. Or perhaps there was a gap in the curtains... but there didn't seem to be. There was no explanation of what it could be. But all I can say is that I didn't feel alone. I tried my yes/no conversations technique, and I couldn't make out any pulls at all, nothing. But as I lay there pondering, an inner knowing came to me that they are there for me and that the overriding message is to get well.

20.06.12 I am still feeling the kneading, pulling and fizzing in various parts of my body. I haven't really got to grips with what is going on. Anna talks of a higher level of consciousness. I pretend to understand what she means but really, I have no idea. It's very exciting to think that I can talk to my spiritual team.

I cannot resist trying to communicate, so I try again.

I drop into a deep state of peace and stillness – perhaps this is the different level of consciousness. I clear my brain of thoughts. It is getting easier to do this. It is a blissful place to be, like deep in an ocean, very calm and safe. I was getting excited about where this could take me and thought it would be useful to really hone this skill. However, I began running out of questions, and I also began to ask myself whether it was me and I was making it all up. Was my own body doing strange things again to give me the answers I already knew? I wondered if I was interpreting the answers, and so getting the pull up or down response was just a figment of my imagination. All the questions I had asked were to do with this dimension, the Earth, and the people around me, so I thought I'd find out a bit more about who I was asking.

As I lay there deeply relaxed in this stillness with my eyes closed, I got a sense of two energies to my right and one to my left. The energy was more of a heat haze, not the pixelated distortions from the hospital room. I had the sense that the one to the left felt important.

I began to feel special. I began with easy questions like 'Should I be a healer?' and get an obvious pull down. My connection seemed very strong indeed, and the answers were clear. I then asked, 'Am I the second coming, another Jesus?' and I get a very definite NO. A wave of a mix of disappointment and elation came over me, but my ego was getting in the way.

So, from what I had learnt already, these heat hazes could be my spiritual guides, part of my team that looks after me. I feel unsure about the existence of a God. Is there one? From what I had learnt so far, it wasn't apparent.

All was going well, so I decided I would ask the ultimate question, and I warn them that I am going to ask the ultimate question.

I brace myself and I say to them that I understand I have a guardian angel and guides; they exist, and are with me and I fully believe in you and your existence – I thank them for all they do for me, and a wave of heat blanketed over me. 'But tell me, is there a God?'

Oh, my goodness, what happened next was mind-blowing, literally. I was calmly waiting for either a pull down or pull up but instead, I got a loud, slamming, crashing sound, like a clashing of symbols. It was *bang, bang, bang* in my head. Not at all what I was expecting. I was shocked and panicked, and tears welled up in my eyes. Immediately, I began with a ream of apologies – 'I'm so sorry I have upset you, I'm sorry, I'm sorry. Please don't leave me.' As I asked that question, the energy to my left dramatically disappeared, leaving a hollow gap, but the other two energies remained.

I was ashamed of myself. How dare I question God? But it left no doubt in my mind: God does exist in some form or other. Wow.

It was three days before I tried any communication again.

Gigaro Beach in the South of France

3. PROPOSAL

The best and most beautiful things in the world cannot be seen
or even touched – they must be felt with the heart
Helen Keller

I am a little shell-shocked after my questioning God incident. I feel small and a little wounded, but I pick myself up and start looking forward. The course has to be finished, with catching up from the missed seminar, the final seminars to do and then a dissertation. I also have to do a practice treatment on a tutor. I work flat out at finishing the course and winding up Scribble House. I just really cannot wait to get started with my new career.

The treatment on a tutor is a little scary, but I put my trust in the fact that the tutors want us all to pass and so if we struggle, I am sure they will help out. I do my one on Nicky and I tell her that I could sense something going on with her right knee. She hadn't told me there was a problem with her knee, so I was pleased to have spotted it. My dissertation is well received too, and I pass with flying colours!

In the meantime, and in between recuperating from the operation and finishing the course, we go to the South of

France in the car to spend some time with friends.

My favourite film of all time is Johnny Depp's 1993 film, Benny and Joon. It has good music, it's fun, there's suspense and emotion and above all it's got a happy ending. Richard, due to there being love in the film, and his struggle with emotion, refuses to watch it. So, in my head, I have been rehearsing when he eventually asks me to marry him, that I will say, 'Only if you watch Benny and Joon.'

Richard suggests we go for a three-hour walk, up a steep hill through the pine forest to a small church on top of the hill overlooking St Tropez. Now, although I have been recovering speedily in the last ten weeks, a three-hour uphill walk would wipe me out for the next day, so I flatly refused! Unbeknown to me, he had planned for champagne to be in the church on top of the hill and his plan was to ring the bell in the chapel following asking me the question I had been waiting for, for a long time. After my putting my foot down, another plan had to be made!

Instead, we went to Gigaro beach and walked along the coastal path, winding our way through the rocks and along the sea edge. We found a log, sat on it and looked out across the ocean. It was a beautiful spot. It was here that he asked me to marry him. He didn't get down on one knee because he probably wouldn't have been able to get up, but he did ask me in a very loving way to spend the rest of my life with him. I thought I would have felt the tension in him, and had an inclination that it was about to happen so that I could have planned my reply, but I didn't.

Instead, I burst into tears, hugged him and said absolutely YES!! I couldn't stop grinning and I honestly don't think I have ever felt so happy. We had champagne and an incredible seafood lunch with our friends, Timmy and Weena, back at their stunning house. It was only later that day when it dawned on me that I hadn't said what I had planned. To this date, he still hasn't watched Benny and Joon.

We are married in Owston church with 120 of our family and friends, old and new, from far and wide. My nephew, Caspar, flew in from New York which was so kind and of course, Timmy and Weena came from France. It was as much a multi-faith service as we were allowed to do by the Christian church, and we had a gospel choir blasting out *Oh Happy Day* and we really couldn't have been happier. Digby did a reading and Alice gave a speech at the reception which had everyone rolling about in laughter.

Now was the start of the rest of my life!

Grounding in our own energy and surrounded by a Merkaba

4. SPIRITUAL JOURNEY

You are going to create options of reality and bring them to the mass consciousness of the planet. You will do this by first doing it for yourself, creating an inner peace and inner love by accepting who you are and all that you have done in life and all that has been done to you in life. You will accept and integrate these things because you will know they have been exactly the situations necessary to bring you into this final stage of anchoring light.
– Bringers of the Dawn by Barbara Marciniak

So where am I now? For the past ten years, I've been treating clients and learning all the time. I now don't mind being called a wacky healer. Thinking back to my sessions with Ralph when he told me I was a channel for healing, my journey has been long and fascinating. The previous prediction about not being rich certainly came true but I am rich in so many other ways; I'm comfortable and I have enough and all that I need and so for me that is enough.

Thinking back to the meditation that I had around twelve years ago when I saw a meeting of people or people sitting around a table that certainly came true. In my overenthusiasm for being a Craniosacral Therapist having joined the Association that monitors and regulates the various schools that teach the therapy, I decided to join the trustees and get more involved which ultimately led to me becoming the Chairman of the Association which I did for two years.

The pulling down for yes and up for no, I continued to practise but after reading *The Emotion Code* by Dr Bradley Nelson, I now use a different form of technique. Some people dowse using a crystal on a chain which will tell them yes and no answers but after reading *The Emotion Code*, (which I cannot recommend highly enough I think everyone should read it), I now have an extremely useful technique, a form of dowsing. Standing upright, I allow my body to sway; forward for a yes and backwards for a no.

The Emotion Code sway test is very useful for use within client sessions, on your pets or even for yourself. I communicate with my dogs by using the sway test method and it is fascinating what I learn from them. I also use it to test if I need my supplements; I have around six that I test for; occasionally I need all six but generally, I only need a couple, if any. This ensures my body does not get overloaded with vitamins that it cannot absorb. One thing I have learnt is to ask myself rather than assume that if the packet says you should, then you should! If there's one book that you should read, I cannot stress enough, that this book, *The Emotion Code*, should be a priority on your list. It will help you to understand that you have got a soul, a higher governing form of intelligence within you, that can help you with your journey here on Earth. This technique really will help you. It does not replace your natural intuition but can be used alongside it.

I have learned so much from my hundreds of clients; each session is different and each session for the client is different. Session number two will be completely different to the first session. They learn too on their journey, and I learn about the bigger picture. Working with clients has given me clarity regarding suicide, gender and race.

As I have said before, I feel deeply that I was a black man in a previous life which makes me think therefore about gender and race; none of this should be an issue in an ideal world. Think about it, we are bodies inhabiting a soul and the soul keeps coming back and reincarnates to teach us life lessons. We have been creating our own realities. Now there will become a time when you have learned so much and understand so much that you will not need to go through the reincarnations of learning life lessons. This is when you have a deep inner knowledge, you have no need to prove what you feel or are being told because you will know it on a deep intuitive level almost as if you have always known it. This is what I call l my deep inner knowing. When this happens you will live your life intuitively; you will know what to do, what to think, how to be, how to connect with your innermost feelings and how to live your life in a successful way, not in a monetary way, but in a deeply contented way; wholesome, fully integrated with your soul and connected to source, from where you came originally.

For many years I have been having a vivid vision of a baby being killed. Now I'm not going to describe the exact details because I feel as if I've moved on from that and I don't want to put energy into that scene that has haunted me for decades. Each time I saw a baby, I would have a flash of this scene in my head. In the early years of my work, I would also have this vision when I was treating babies. I cleared this haunting by using various techniques such as Craniosacral therapy, shamanism and hypnotherapy which cleared away the past life memory of me witnessing the death of my baby. Once this image faded to a scene with no emotion attached to it, I could then move forward in my life with regards to treating and even seeing babies. There is no way of proving that this actually happened but I assure you I have an inner knowing that it did, because it had affected me so deeply for so long.

We are all on different journeys so we will all experience different things in order to wake up. I had a spiritual awakening back on the 1st January 2011 which woke me up from living a life centred around money and jobs. My journey needed the experiences that I have had in order for me to become more enlightened, your journey will need different experiences. All I would say to you is to open your mind so that you can receive information that is coming to you. Open your eyes so that you may see the information that is being shown to you. Open your ears in case you hear something that is being said to you. Use your other sense, which is intuition, that will also be giving you information. Trust that intuition is very powerful. It is a message from your higher self or your soul and it is there to help you on your journey on this planet.

We are made up of energy held together by force. Everything that we say and think is a form of energy. There was a Japanese doctor, Dr Emoto, who did experiments with water using energy and thought. He proved that human consciousness could affect the molecular structure of water. A group of people surrounding a glass of water sending love to the water by saying or thinking sentences like 'I love you, I need you, you sustain me, you're delicious.' This energy has an effect on that water. When that water is frozen and put under a microscope it is possible to see the beautiful crystals that those words have influenced the water. Each word forms a differently shaped water crystal. Water found in different parts of the world also had different crystal structures. Now, I find this fascinating. Just think for a moment: how full of water are we? We are more than 70% water so think about the effect that all words and thoughts and any information that we may be receiving either via the television, social media or newspapers has an effect on our bodies. Think also how the world is also 70% water and what is happening within our world and how it is affecting the water. Dr Emoto went on further with the experiments using negative words on a similar glass of water. The group of people would sit around and say to the water, 'You are stagnant, you are ugly, you are disgusting, I detest you,' and other similar words. Under a microscope, there are no crystal formations whatsoever. If you'd like to look more into this then check out Doctor Emoto's water experiments on YouTube or read his book The Hidden Messages in Water.

Some of us can see energy like a heat haze that you would see in a desert. Sometimes people see little lights, either black or white, swirling about in the sky, others will see colours in different layers. Some people see auras around the physical human body. One client said that they could see a heat haze in the treatment room and described it. It is something that she has seen for the whole of her life. When I explained that what she was actually seeing was energy, she was so relieved because as a child she thought she had a problem with her eyes. Her eyes were checked many times and no problem was diagnosed.

In 2023, a huge shift in our individual frequencies took place on this planet. Some people would have been unaware of this, and others knew what was going on. Some of you felt the effects of this frequency upgrade and were confused about why you are feeling anxious, wired, or even in pain. We are all here experiencing different histories, different stories and relationships and all having different experiences that all our souls need to have in order for us to progress on a spiritual level. Some of us live in the 3D, the 3rd dimension. These people tend to be concerned with where the money is coming from how big the house is, the importance of working in a job whether they enjoy it or not, your car and the next fancy holiday.

This used to be me. Most of those people are being awakened too, and many of them are very confused. If you recognise yourself as a 3D person and you are having dreams about losing all your irrelevant material possessions, then maybe your dream is trying to tell you something: that life is more than possessions. Listen to your dreams. If you are reading this book and you are living in a 3D existence, then think about the reason why you are reading this book.

Take time out of your day to rest and recuperate. Take time to turn off your brain and your thoughts and your ego. Eckhart Tolle's book *The Power of Now* is a good book to start with. There are techniques within this book that will show you how to switch off the monkey brain that likes to be in control. There are also guided meditations on YouTube that you can listen to. When you manage to free your brain, you begin to look within and you will begin to receive messages regarding what you should be doing and how you should be living your life.

When you live in the 4D world this is when you realise that the 3D world is not where you want to be, and it is time to stand up to those in charge within the 3D world. It is time to either shout from the rooftops about the injustices going on in the world or speak your truth sitting around your kitchen table at home; either way, it's about speaking your truth. Often, there is anger surrounding the 4D level of human. If you bear in mind Dr Emoto's water experiments, you will be aware of how important it is not to be negative, angry or fearful. All these negative emotions will influence your physical body, and ultimately, your health.

When you live in a 5D way, you will be trusting that whatever is going on in the world is happening for a reason. When you live in a 5D world your frequency, like your radio station, is working at a high and purely loving level. Your thoughts and words will come from your heart and will be only positive. You will begin to realise how the negativity that surrounds us in this world can have an effect on your highly tuned and sensitive energetic body. In fact, any negativity, whether it is from listening to someone's conversation, reading something or watching it on the TV, will have a physical effect on you. Listen to your body, it is telling you about the way you are living. This is commonly known as the three states of consciousness.

Thinking back to the death of Diana, the Princess of Wales, the shock and sadness throughout the world was palpable. You probably know the feeling of when you walk into a room full of people you can get a sense of the energy of that room and it can stop you in your tracks. You may say, 'Whoa, what's happening here?' Similarly, if you walk into a room full of very happy people emitting joyful light and happy energy, you will feel the effects of that energy.

I'm sure you all know of friends or colleagues or even members of your family who, after you have been with them for a while, will have had an impact on the energy of your body. When you realise this, you are on your journey into understanding you as an energetic soul within a physical body. You will realise how important it is that your energy and your soul and your body needs to be working in harmony in order to function optimally. Just keep listening to what your body is telling you.

The expression of 'going with the flow' is something we should all be doing. If you are finding something difficult to accomplish, then you should stop forcing that journey. When something is easy and things start slotting into place, there is no need to change, you are on the right path. If your life has become a struggle, it means you are heading in the wrong direction, something needs to change in your life.

When I say or think something that is aligned with what I need to know or act upon, I get a cold, tingly whoosh that descends down my body, particularly down my legs. Listen to your own body and see if you too get the same sensation. It is a confirmation that you are on the right track, a confirmation from your soul.

Keep listening to your inner voice, external information, sway test results, your gut instinct.

Keep listening.

Ascending to the light

5. AFTER WE DIE

Death is not the greatest loss in life. The greatest loss is what dies inside us while we live.
— Norman Cousins

Death was not the end; it was the new beginning that created a circle of life.
— 'Discovering your past lives', Gloria Chadwick

Clients

During the last ten years, I have had many, many clients who during the session will have a recollection of a past life. As a practitioner, I rarely see a past life. But so many of my clients have had experiences, visions, a sense, a feeling, or a deep understanding of a past life that they believe it to be absolutely true. I've had so many of these clients that I fully believe that a great many of us have had past lives and that these lives should be considered during our current incarnation. I, myself, believe that I was once a black man. I also feel that I have had an experience of my own child being murdered and I also get a sense that I have died of starvation in a gutter. It is not up to me to prove that these things have happened because often it is impossible to prove.

Dr Jim B Tucker heads a team of researchers at the University of Virginia, USA, proving the memories of previous lives of children. His research is based on more than 2,500 cases and he has written many books. One I suggest is *Life before Life*. I do not need evidence, I will leave that up to the team in Virginia. For me, I have an inner knowledge that I know in my heart and soul it is true. Similarly, my clients have this same inner knowing; these experiences within a session or a meditation are real to them.

Not all past life experiences are related to a death in a past life. Some will be an experience within that lifetime. Some of my clients have had chains around their ankles and visions of them being African slaves. Some have had cannonballs in their legs, arrows in their shoulders, hangings, executions, loss of limbs, daggers or spears in their side. So many clients have had such a variety of different experiences I fully believe that for most people on this planet, they have had a past life or many lives.

There are, on the other hand, many of the younger generations who are new souls, people who've had no experience before of any previous life. This may explain the struggles some of the younger generation are going through. This subject is investigated in great depth by Dolores Cannon in her book *The Three Waves of the Volunteers and the New Earth,* which I recommend for those a little further on in their spiritual journey. See the back of this book for a list of further reading.

In the summer of 2020, my most precious dog, a yellow Labrador Quito, became very ill. She lost weight and was very tired. A growth in her gut, which I had initially thought was something that she'd eaten, turned out to be a tumour which was inoperable. The vet delivered this information to me whilst Quito was still under general anaesthetic. She asked me what I wanted to do, whether I wanted to allow her to die now or whether I wanted her to return home for a few more days. She told me she would not have long to live. My decision was to bring her round, return her home and make her last few days as comfortable as possible. I also wanted to explain to her, using my various sway test techniques that I had learned with *The Emotion Code,* what was happening for her so that she understood. I personally also needed time to prepare for losing someone so special.

Her last three weeks were made very comfortable. She had incredibly spoiling food and gentle walks that she could manage. She and I had a very special time indeed. Using the sway test method, I explained to her what was going to happen at the vet and what would happen to her. She appeared to be understanding and resigned to the fact this was the end of her life in physical form.

We drove to the vet and she seemed happy and content with what was going on. Strict rules about social distancing were in place at that time. We lay her in the boot of the car and with an extended lead delivering the lethal dose for euthanasia, the vet slowly delivered the poison. I asked the vet whether I could stay with her until her soul had left her body; she confirmed that that was okay. I feel this is something that we should all be aware of. We should bear this in mind when anyone we love, human or animal, departs from this physical realm. I sat with Quito, still palpating her energy within the technically dead physical body for 25 minutes after she'd been pronounced dead. Because I can palpate energy, I can feel the energy in her and then I actually saw her egg-shaped, four-foot, hazy-looking soul leave her body; it paused and hovered just above her body, and then whoosh in a sweep, like a Nike tick, headed up to the sky. I then touched her body, and there was nothing left. Even though going through this process was extremely difficult, I felt honoured and privileged to be able to be with her until her soul actually departed. This is something we could all learn from.

Occasionally, when I'm dealing with a client whose issues may be to do with a deceased animal, particularly a dog, and the client is comfortable with me speaking this way, I will call in Quito so that she may reassure and comfort either my client or the deceased pet.

So what happens when we die? Sometimes, people have near-death experiences and will report going down tunnels of white light, in fields of flowers, in clouds, and many different experiences. Because we're all on different energetic frequencies within this planet, it determines where we go in our next realm. Some souls, particularly if they have no religious belief, may get trapped on this plane, like a ghost.

Occasionally, within a client session, I get a sense of an attached soul, a soul that has piggybacked onto the energy field of another human. Generally, this is not something to be concerned about, but sometimes it affects the host.

Gillian

Gillian came to see me, and was my first experience of a past life, or rather past lives. She was a slight 65 years old, with beautiful pale skin and light grey, almost white hair. To be honest, I humoured her by listening and showing my understanding face. She told me during filling in the client history form that she struggled with her neck because of a past life trauma when she was at Auschwitz.

Sometimes she would release things from this lifetime, like falling off a wall. And almost every time she came, it seemed we uncovered another life. She was a client for almost three years and then went off to train in craniosacral therapy because she loved the treatment so much.

We had a cannonball in her leg which resulted in an amputation, a knife in her neck, a scene from the Battle of Boscastle, the Boer War, the Battle of Trafalgar, a spear in her pelvis, dagger in her ribs and many times when she was abused. She proudly announced to me that it was her mission to clear all the baggage her soul was carrying, which came not only from this life but all her multitude of previous lives, so that she can come back in the next life to do what her soul wishes to do.

Fiona

Fiona first came to see me in September 2018. She is married and they have three children. She came because she was generally exhausted, recovering from a recent bout of shingles, and feeling anxious and overwhelmed. She said she was 'feeling slightly out of control.' She struggled to get to sleep and had IBS. She'd had many but small childhood injuries, some requiring a general anaesthetic; her children were all born naturally, and she herself was a forceps delivery. Her parents divorced when she was in her teens, which she found very unsettling, and her brother was a drug addict, which had a profound impact on all members of the family. This was her first experience of CST.

The session began with me at her feet. We were just settling into it when she started heavy breathing and looked in distress. Her system felt very dense and something was going on that wasn't the usual tissues letting go. I checked in with her to see if she was OK and she said yes. It felt like something important and big, so I stayed at her feet now with hands-off, and kept reassuring her that she was here in the room and that she was safe. She continued to shake and breathe heavily for the whole session time of forty minutes. She didn't want to talk about it during the session but afterwards, she revealed everything. It was a surprise to me to say the least.

Fiona saw herself as a man, a fighter pilot in a plane, the plane crashed and it was dark; she felt as if she was drowning. It was very intense and we both had a feeling that something was being unearthed, that it was big and that it would take

116

some time. I had to assure her that this was not CST in the norm; her system or her soul was letting go of a past memory.

Here comes the question, 'How do you feel about reincarnation?' I casually said that it could be a past life death her soul had experienced. This, she felt, was true; she had an inner knowing that that was indeed what had been happening. I thought this would be the last I heard from her, I thought she had been disturbed by what had happened and the possibility of reincarnation and that she would never return.

But she did come back. A week later, she told me that she had a feeling of dread lifting and had been shaking for four days, then it all stopped and she felt so great. We start the next session, hands-off throughout; it's like her body knws what it can get rid of whilst it is in my presence. And it can't wait to start. Again, she is shaking and heavy-breathing, but this time she talks during the releasing. She said that her death felt like she didn't want to die; she (he) died too soon.

I was in love... There's a young woman hanging out the washing... I can see a cottage... I'm crashing... It's stormy... The sea is rough... I'm drowning.

Suddenly, everything was calm, her breathing settled and her body stilled. I thought that it was all over and that was it when she began convulsing, her right arm twisting and struggling to breathe. I asked her to think of a place where she felt safe, her favourite spot, to ground her and bring her more into the present, but the place she chose was in the house of her previous life, not where I had wanted her to choose really.

I'm birthing into this world… No, I don't want to come… It's too soon…

Now, this was an absolute first for me! I am trying to react as if this is perfectly normal and not at all weird! Trying to stay calm and steady in my voice.

I thought that must be her last session; she must be totally freaked by this. But instead, she began researching past lives, whatever she could on the internet. She read *Many Lives, Many Masters* by Dr Weizz and really began to 'get' her life. She confessed before our next session that she had attempted suicide three times in her teens. She had had a happy childhood but just had a feeling that she didn't want to be here. She now has a happy life with a wonderful husband and three gorgeous children, but still, she had a sense that she didn't really want to be here. Now this feeling all made perfect sense. She had died too soon, when she really didn't want to die and had so much to live for and was very much in love. Then she rebirthed and felt it was all too soon; she came back too soon. It was such a relief to understand herself. This knowledge gave her permission to let it go, to allow herself to be who she really is in this life and to realise why she had had these feelings in the first place.

She had several more sessions. Each one was hands-off, each time releasing a little more of both the death and the birth. In one of the sessions, she could smell the smoke, the plane on fire, the pilot behind her grabbing her shoulder and she could feel the heat of the fire. She coughed for five days after that treatment. However, her body was beginning to feel like the energy was in it and not disassociated, but more embodied. In fact, she was a new woman, more confident, more grounded, more centred and more in control of her feelings. And with a deep, deep understanding of her life, her lives.

It is interesting to know that when a past life comes up, we must not assume that that is the only release needed and it has gone. Just as with physical issues in the system, the releasing can go on over several sessions.

Harriet

I had a client called Harriet, who had been on holiday with a dear friend recently. She came for treatment after feeling extremely out of sorts. Her friend's husband, who two years prior to that, had died and Harriet had been at the hospital bedside with her friend whilst he died. I got a sense that there was another energy in the treatment room and suggested to Harriet that it could be possible that her friend's husband's soul had decided to attach itself to her. My thinking is initially the soul piggybacked onto his wife, not wanting to leave her. The soul then saw an opportunity to attach to a new host, Harriet.

It was a strange feeling in the treatment room, a sense of real unease. My intuition said one thing and my sway test said another. Generally, in these circumstances, there's some entity either attached or in the room that needs dealing with. Harriet lay down on the couch and I asked her just to remain still, calm and to tune into her breathing. I then tried to talk to the attached soul. It felt like the soul was hiding. In my head the words *'what the f**k'* came up three times. This wasn't something that had happened to me before. So, I asked Harriet what was the deceased man's religious belief. She said, 'Oh, he was an atheist'.

I then told her what I was hearing, that I had '*what the f**k*' said over and over again in my head. She said that was exactly the type of thing he would say. This confirmed what we were dealing with. So, I then spent the rest of the session talking with him, explaining how the soul needs to go to the light in order to move up to the next level and carry out the duties the soul is required to do having left this physical realm. I checked in all the time with him to make sure he was comfortable with it and he was. So I then used a technique to help the soul move on, and we felt his energy disappear from the room. Occasionally, the soul is not ready to move on and stays for longer on this plane. That is OK if the host is not being affected by it.

Sometimes, souls are not actually attached but they are sending messages to the person still here in this physical plane. Adeline's son, Drew, who died two years previously having taken his own life, often came through during a session to let us know he is there. When Adeline went to visit a psychic, the psychic told her what Drew needed to say and she repeated it to me. Drew had told his mother that he can't see a human form, he only sees the glowing light of the soul energy. He said if her energy is not shining brightly enough, he cannot see it.

This was quite a revelation for us. Adeline had been in deep grief for the past two years and was struggling to come to terms with his death. This made her really determined to move forward so that her own soul's energy frequency could shine as brightly as possible so that her son could see her. This was one of those absolute revelation moments that often happen during or after sessions. It makes perfect sense, and it is something that we should all know about.

Jessica

Jessica is a sporty blond 20-year-old who rides horses. She also falls off them occasionally. She has a very responsive body and quickly resolves held trauma of two fractured vertebrae in just two sessions. She came to me with a permanently sore lower back, stiff shoulders and tightness at the base of her skull. Once the trauma within the bones was allowed to let go with a fluttery and fuzzy feeling, her body as a whole felt as if it had discharged and rebalanced itself. It is highly unusual that her treatment plan ended up with only three sessions.

She comes back as and when she needs it. But her system has a sense of fragility so if she has any upsets to it, either physically or emotionally, then she's back visiting me for sessions. She knows and understands how to keep her body in the optimum of health and that is all I can ever ask of any client. Just understand and listen to what it needs and help it out. We all need to take responsibility of our own health.

What is so wonderful is that CST is bespoke to each client. As Bessel van der Kolk says, 'The body holds the score.' There is an inner wisdom within us that knows how to self-heal. Life's traumas and tribulations get in the way and it can't do what it is supposed to do.

After all, you wouldn't buy a car and expect it to be running years later, with no servicing in between. Our body, the vessel within our soul, needs looking after and the relationship between the two needs to be in perfect harmony. This is what craniosacral therapy can rebalance.

Charlie

Sometimes when I treat a client, I get a sense of very powerful energy, something strong yet sensitive. Perhaps it's an old soul with an important job to do during this time on Earth. These clients are described as empaths and today in 2023, I am seeing more and more of this type of client; someone who can feel and sense the emotions of others, who is highly intuitive, who needs alone time and to replenish in nature. They may cry a lot and find cities difficult places to go to.

Charlie was certainly one of those. He was a university student who had fallen into a wall and been concussed. An MRI scan showed nothing, but he was presenting with migraines and digestion issues. He had a painful left shoulder which had been troubling him for years.

The real problem for Charlie wasn't the fall against a wall that caused him extreme headaches; his issues were buried much deeper with abandonment issues from being sent away to boarding school and two of his friends committing suicide, one of whom was his best friend. The pain in his shoulder, was in fact coming from his heart. He was also an empath so had a sensitively heightened energy field.

He had nine sessions in all; the first ones at weekly intervals and then the gaps lengthening out. The first session, he was an overloaded and overwhelmed energetic mess. Once the nervous system had been calmed down, the releasing between the sessions often involved shaking, heartache and crying. I helped him in between to learn how to manage these very sensitive reactions himself. He carried a stone in his pocket to help with grounding, learned to control his breathing, did visualisations particularly of his safe place and learnt how to protect his energy field. And because he is an empath, he felt like he was releasing for his whole family as well as the family of his friends who took their lives. He was living their pain too.

It was a steep learning curve for him. His mother contacted me towards the end of his treatment plan and told me his journey of recovery had had a profound effect on the whole family. He now understands his body, the way it reacts and is in full control.

I am very proud of Charlie and all that he has achieved on his healing journey. Like so many of my clients, he needed to work out the things his body needs in order to function at the optimum of health. I am merely a facilitator for this learning; an onlooker, someone who triggers a client's ability to heal themselves; it is a humbling experience.

Helena

Helena is a 48-year-old administrator with two children. She is married but struggles with stress, diagnosed adrenal fatigue and feels emotionally vulnerable. She has been grinding her teeth since she was seven years old and as a consequence has overdeveloped muscles in her jaw. She is constantly having problems with her teeth cracking and her whole head feels tense and tight. Her digestion is sluggish and she doesn't sleep well because of her jaw. She wears a retainer at night.

My first thought when we are going through her history, is why would she be grinding her teeth at the age of seven? What was happening in her life to make her do this? Her father was in the army and moved a lot and from the age of seven she was away at boarding school. At 17 she had quinsy (a type of tonsilitis) and septicaemia (blood poisoning) which meant she was on antibiotics for 9 months, she then had a tonsillectomy. Since then, she has been suffering from digestive problems. She suffered from chronic fatigue syndrome in her early 20's which was so severe that she became paralysed and for a short time, became blind. She recovered slowly over three years.

All these things that have happened to her will have influenced the physiology of her body. When treating someone, I do not treat the symptoms; I treat the whole person, focusing on the health within the body and freeing it up so it can rebalance itself. Our bodies are designed to self-heal and if they are functioning in a strong and balanced way, the body naturally self-heals.

Helena lies down, facing upwards and I begin the session as I usually do, from the feet. Her body feels dense and tight, from the outer edge to the very core. I sense that all her tissues, whether they are organs or connective tissue have a solid and held feeling. Her body begins to soften by tingling gently and throughout the session I move to different positions around her body, spending around half the time at her head. I tune into the jaw, the TMJs (temporomandibular joints, just in front of the ears) and the pterions (a junction of three bones in the skull, just behind the ears). She notices pulls, tingling and sensations all over her body and has a sense of feeling lighter, like a weight is beginning to lift from her shoulders.

She tells me later that she burped all the way home. Burping is one of the signs that a body is releasing, although very few of my clients usually burp!

When Helena returns the following week she said her jaw felt a lot better, she felt as if she was struggling to breathe and then cried for hours with a friend. She wasn't sure why she was crying but recognised that it came from deep within. We do a similar session to the initial one but also tune into the vagus nerve (which runs from the head, to the gut via the stomach and pancreas). There's a fuzziness and a sense of softening and relaxing from the nerve and the organs along it. There was also a big heat release from her diaphragm.

Two weeks later, she reports that her jaw is still improving (but not there yet), her gut felt better, and her digestion had improved. With this session, I had a sense that I was getting deeper into her very being. If you imagine the body like a swimming pool, the first two sessions were on or near the surface, now it felt like I was deeper in the swimming pool. We did more release work at the shoulders, the throat, the top of the neck and then the TMJs and jaw. She cried too when I put my hands on her heart as memories flooded back to her, and the stomach and gut, which had a sense of being numb, gave way to fizzing and tingling.

She cried in the car all the way home and had a whole day of heightened anxiety. That dispersed the following day and left her feeling more content and sure of herself. At the next session, we continued with shoulders, heart, along the spine, the vagus nerve and of course, her head and jaw.

After this session, which was her fourth, Helena felt brave enough to sleep without her gum guard for the first time since she was seven years old. It was only for one night, though.

Following the fifth session, she has the courage to take out the gum guard for good and tells me how she is getting her mind to focus on the good parts of her body rather than any discomfort.

Her sessions reduced to monthly ones for the next three and now she comes as and when she senses her body is in need of rebooting – in fact, she describes it as 'Control/Alt/Delete' for the body.

Alison

Alison is a 42-year-old Mum of two with two stepchildren. She's married, lives in Durham and works from home.

She suffered from stress, anxiety, fatigue, irritable bowel syndrome (IBS) and had recently been hospitalised with a panic attack that had lasted 24 hours. She contacted me because although she had been living with these symptoms, she had now developed tinnitus for the past ten weeks. She searched online for help with tinnitus and read that CST could help.

The only problem was that Alison could not leave her house. When she was born, her 17-year-old mother couldn't cope, so she spent the first six months with a foster carer. Her Mum took her back when she was six months old, and she never had a relationship with her father. Even at an early age, children can sense abandonment, and this was a large part of her story. Her Mum struggled to cope and so Alison went to live with her grandmother. She described her childhood as difficult and left home when she was 13 years old; she had four jobs and managed to look after herself.

She struggled with maintaining relationships; one boyfriend physically abused her. The abuse was also a big part of her story. She suffered from depression in her early 20's and began taking the medication citalopram. She suffered many ear and throat infections and had her tonsils out when she was 22. She also had damaged her knee when she fell on the kitchen floor a few years earlier.

I agreed to give Alison CST sessions in her home. As I have said before, with a client, I am not treating the symptoms, I treat the whole person.

At the first session, her energy throughout and surrounding her body was unsettled and had a shaky agitated feel about it. I spent most of the session at her feet allowing her nervous system to settle the overwhelm. I also spent time with my hand on her adrenals which are the centre for the distribution of adrenaline and cortisol around the body. When a system feels overwhelmed like hers, often the adrenals are on constant discharge. This can lead to adrenal fatigue. Her heart and her head felt way too blocked and trapped for me to even put my hands on.

Alison said she had a sense she was being cuddled like a baby. I knew there was a deep fragility to her system and that I had to take things slowly. We talked during the session of having a safe place and to think of it regularly using all her senses. This is so important and a fundamental need for a human to feel safe. Once a person begins to feel safe in the world, the healing happens quicker.

The second session was a week later, again at her house. She said she had felt grounded, positive and happy and that it had lasted for four days. Then doom set in again. There had been no change in the tinnitus. When I put my hands on her, her system felt completely different. The fluidity of her body was smoother and stronger feeling. I could get my hands on her head and briefly at her heart. She could get a sense of patterns of tension lifting from parts of her body and it was feeling lighter. It was after this session that she managed to walk to the nearby park.

During the sessions and in the first few days afterwards, Alison's body released more of the physical manifestations of the deeply held trauma in her body. Sometimes she knew what it was related to and other times her body would release and we would have no idea. It doesn't matter. Each week, she felt more positive, calmer and happier. The tinnitus was still there but was reduced and intermittent.

After the third, we extended the gap between the sessions. Now when treating her, her energy and body were integrated so that I could palpate the held tension in various parts of her body like the heart, diaphragm, her throat, the vagus nerve, the jaw, the ears and various bones of the cranium. She had several recollections of early memories as different holding patterns let go. When her right knee released shock in a holding that extended from her knee to the top of her head during her fifth session, the full unravelling began. It was gentle but profound. She had a cry and felt liberated.

On the fifth session, Alison managed the journey to my clinic over an hour away. She had been experiencing heartache that ached out down her arms three times a day. The tinnitus had gone for a few days but although back, was now at such a low level that she forgot about it. It is not ruling her life anymore and she's noticing good things around her. The relationships with her husband, her children and step-children had all improved. During this appointment, she was mainly releasing from her heart, then her head, which she described as a blackness lifting and rising above her, which was immediately replaced by white light.

She felt confident to leave a longer gap between the sessions. Slowly, over the coming weeks, the heartache ached out altogether; she realised that she was loved and that she was happy. Her relationship with her mother improved, she had a newfound confidence and had, with the approval of her doctor, come off the medication altogether. Her skin and hair looked healthier too.

She comes to me every couple of months and yes, there is more to resolve. Each time we clear a bit more from her system, but she is in control of herself, her physical body and her emotions. In one of her 'maintenance' sessions, we talked about her blocked pelvis. She had the blocked, bloated feeling all her life. I checked in with her system using the dowsing sway test, and it confirmed that it was linked to a past life. It was tricky to work out what exactly had happened in a past life to store that energy in her gut but something significant had happened. It could well have been more than one past life with gut issues. We both felt the confirming shivers as we talked about what could have been. She said it felt like a heavy dark energy being pulled out of her. She left feeling light, floaty and free. It was a very profound treatment.

Above all, she now has a deep understanding of her journey in a human body and how this life and past lives have affected her development as a person. Moreover, she understands when her mind and body is in need of help and she knows exactly what to do. It may be exercise or it may be a soak in an Epsom salts bath; she understands what her body requires and she continues to grow from strength to strength.

Babies

Babies can respond very quickly to CST, particularly to help clear birth trauma. I love to treat babies as their energy fields feel so open and willing to respond. Sometimes, their discomfort (pain, acid reflux, bonding issues) is resolved in just one session but more often a few. They have an inner wisdom and I always speak to them very slowly, and it is as if they understand me.

I am still on my journey and learning every day. I wanted to share with you all I have learned. I have had the honour and the privilege of working with clients who reveal to me more than I could ever have learned on my own. I am truly grateful to all my clients for everything they have taught me. I now have a much greater understanding of what life is about and this is what I wish to share with you. You probably will not believe everything that I have told you, but all I wish is for you to open your senses and use your intuition. Listen with your heart and soul, use your gut instinct. All that we need is within us. There is no need to look outside for external help; all the answers are within.

So where do you start? I feel some of you are saying well, I haven't had the buzzy feeling, I haven't had the spiritual awakening, I can't feel the way you can feel because I haven't been given the gift. Eliminate those thoughts from your vocabulary, please, I urge you. Think of your spiritual awakening as reading this book. When you realise your eyes are being opened by simply reading and understanding the words that I am sharing with you, you will realise that you are on your own journey to discovering what life is all about. Everyone goes at different paces; some are faster than me and some are slower. The same will apply to you. All you need to do is slow down your daily life and start listening to your inner voice within you. Speak from your heart, keep your thoughts pure and make your actions from a loving heart-centred place.

There are many guided meditations on YouTube that are a good place to start. There are self-help exercises at the back of this book. Choose which ones suit you. Give each one a go and if it suits you and makes you feel better, then continue to use it regularly. Create a routine in your daily or weekly calendar that includes grounding, breathing and some form of exercise. I have listed books to read at the back of this book, some of which are for those of you who are starting out on your spiritual journey and others are for later in your journey. Think about the fact that we are souls inhabiting a physical body. Think about the importance of being kind to those who struggle with race or gender for when they realise that it is because the soul is not used to being in this body they have taken in this incarnation, they will have a deeper understanding of who they really are.

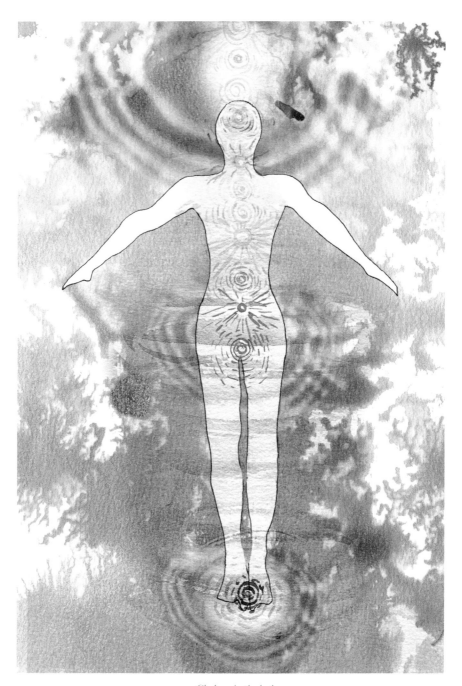

Chakras in the body

6. SELF-HELP EXERCISES

We are not human beings having a spiritual experience, we are spiritual beings having a human experience.
— Teilhard de Chardin

It is during our darkest moments that we must focus to see the light.
— Aristotle Onassis

f you experience discomfort during these exercises, then pause doing them. However, it could be your body releasing what it needs to.

Connecting with your own energy

Some of us are empaths and have wide energy fields, and we are sensitive to other people's energy fields. We often get the sense that we are picking up emotions and even physical sensations from someone else. If you go to visit someone who is depressed and you come away feeling flat, then you have picked their energy up. The same applies when you visit someone who is overjoyed, a bit can rub off on you. This can become a problem if you are living with someone and picking up their energy. If this is you, there are ways you can protect yourself. It is also important to breathe correctly and ground yourself.

Imagine there is a white light above you. Imagine it pouring into the top of your head. It slowly goes down your body and picks up any negative bits that you do not need and then imagine it pouring into the Earth. Do this three times. I do this and then I connect into my heart and say the following out loud, setting my sacred space.

I embrace the sacred space which is an octahedron of light within my heart.
I invite the light to spread throughout my body, through all my chakras and to the edge of my energy fields.
As I sit within a merkaba I ask the angels and archangels to surround me within this light.

I do this every morning. Ask yourself if it is something that would benefit you, if so, add it to your tool kit!

Be aware that thoughts are energy and so negative thoughts will have a negative impact on you. Train yourself to only speak in a positive way. It will make you stronger. For example, turn 'I don't want to be late' into 'I want to be on time'.

Some of us are sensitive to EMF radiation emitted from computers and WIFI. Using an earthing mat (available from Amazon and other retailers) whilst working with a computer will help you. Also, to help with sleep issues, turn off the WIFI at the router at night time. Certainly, do not have a mobile phone by the side of your bed. It will be emitting EMF radiation all night and your body needs to rest. If it goes through a wall, it goes through your body.

Even if we don't classify ourselves as empaths, we still are all connected to each other. We are connected to the environments around us, the people, their words and emotions. We all need to be aware of and look after our own energy field.

Keeping your energy field clear

Adapted from a meditation shared by Adrian Incledon-Webber, Healer/Dowser

Chakras are energy points in the body. Although there are 7 major chakras within the torso, I have used the 12 chakra system. Chakra translates into 'wheel' in Sanskrit; all chakras need to be open and flowing with energy for a balanced mind, body and spirit.

The solar plexus is the yellow area under your breast, the hole between the rib cage, around the stomach area. We use the solar plexus chakra as our centre point. Each colour we breathe in gathers there, at a cellular level and on the out-

I USED TO BE NORMAL

breath, it expands, moving through our physical body, cleansing it. It then continues to the outer edge of our auric field, cleansing that too. Finally, the colour shrinks, giving us the first band around our body. We then start to build up the layers outside that. Just like the layers of an onion.

Sit quietly and take two deep breaths.

- Earth chakra – visualise the colour brown under your feet. As you breathe in, visualise it moving up your legs and body to the solar plexus. As you breathe out visualise it expanding through your body and out to the outer edge of your auric field, cleansing the body and aura. It then shrinks to form a 2" layer of brown around your physical body.
- Base chakra – (coccyx) red, breathe in and bring it up to the solar plexus, breathe it out to the edge of your energy field and then let it drop back to add a second layer around your body
- Sacral chakra – pink, continue as above
- Navel Chakra – orange, continue as above
- Solar Plexus – yellow, breathe in yellow into the solar plexus and breathe out from the same chakra to form another layer
- Heart Chakra – green, on the in-breath take it down to the solar plexus and continue with the layers.
- Thymus or Higher Heart Chakra – aquamarine
- Throat Chakra – dark blue
- Third Eye – purple
- Crown Chakra – white
- Soul Star Chakra – above the crown, breathe in silver and make another layer.

- Divine Gateway Chakra – breathe in gold and make another layer

Your chakras are now cleansed as is your body and auric field. Now, go to your heart and imagine an octahedron (two pyramids on top of each other base to base, like a diamond) of light in it and say: 'I shine my light.'

Again, if this suits you, I recommend that this is done daily, at least once when you wake. If you like you can do it again before going to bed.

Grounding and breathing

When we are swamped with fear or guilt or whatever emotion we are currently experiencing, it can lead to anxiety. We can have a feeling of not being able to cope, of being out of control.

It can be tempting to look over the garden fence to others thinking they are having an easier time than you. The grass is not greener, it is different.

Let's begin with grounding. Take a few minutes, longer if you can, to imagine your feet attached to the Earth – with a chain and anchor or with tree roots, whatever you prefer. Bare feet on the Earth if you can. If not, use your imagination.

Now, focus on your breathing. Slow your breathing down. Listen to it. Make the in-breath through your nose, count it and double the out-breath through your mouth. Keep extending this until 6 ins and 12 outs – longer if you can manage. You can also add to this by imagining your heart filling on the in-breath and emptying on the out-breath.

Connect with a safe place. Create a safe place in your imagination, somewhere you would go to if you were to meditate. It could be somewhere you know or a made-up place. Then slowly using all your senses notice what it looks like, sounds like, feels like, tastes and smells like. Really embody being there.

When you are competent at these three, add them together. Doing this daily will bring some connection and control back into your mind and body.

There are many different breathing exercises available in books or online. The Wim Hoff breathing technique is one I use first thing in the morning and is available as a guided breathing session within 'My Morning Routine' video on the Tanfield Wellness website.

Positivity

Positivity is one of my very favourite self-help techniques. In every sentence, make sure it is positive. This took me around six months to fully achieve.

Change every negative into a positive. 'I don't want to feel flat' needs to be 'I want to be cheerful'. 'I don't want to feel afraid' to 'I want to have courage'. Our minds are incredibly powerful and it doesn't recognise the don'ts and can'ts; so, in fact, you are exacerbating the problem and allowing your mind to draw attention to the very thing you are trying to avoid.

Be grateful, make the most of what you have at this moment in time. Find as many positives as you can and keep reaffirming them. This is what some call 'daily gratitudes' – it's amazing what an effect it can have. If you struggle and can't manage it, just look at the sky, notice how clear it is. The birdsong and how loud it is. A flower and how beautiful it is.

We all, no matter what we are experiencing, will have things to be grateful for.

Grounding and relaxing

When we become quiet, engage with our hearts and feel that the body is a safe space we can tune into our souls. This enables us to experience joy, pleasure, and builds happy hormones. Thoughts are energy and linked to body sensations. Thoughts can free up your body if positive or constrict it when negative.

Tuning into 'you' helps you understand that difficulties and pain don't last forever, and we begin to understand how interconnected the mind, body and soul are.

The body's inner wisdom and natural self-healing comes forth when we tune into ourselves.

Grounding is a health habit to help you when you feel tired, heavy or burdened. Its purpose is to reconnect you with your joy, well-being, allowing negativity to drain away and to return to calm. You will feel the greatest benefit when doing this whilst your bare feet are on the Earth. You can also use an earthing mat; failing that your imagination.

Check-in questions

Ask yourself – how is my body feeling today? What sensation is that feeling giving me? Where is the sensation? If it could speak what would it say?

Take a few deep breaths and say 'It is okay; it's a rough day. This will pass. I now need to come back to my body.'

- Take a posture that is comfortable for you. Since you have named your current feeling or body sense, take a breath and acknowledge where you are.
- Tune your attention and go inside (eyes open or closed).
- Quickly scan your body. If you are sensing irritation, where in your body is it?
- Place your hand on the body area. Take a breath and exhale slowly, melting the experience.
- Feel your feet on the ground.
- Gently push into your feet, as if you're doing a slow walk on the spot.
- Imagine you are pushing away beneath you.
- Now imagine your feet are planted barefoot in the grass or on the ground. Imagine roots coming out of your feet. Focus on slowly breathing out for three minutes.
- Stop, pause and notice your body. Sense and see with your inner imagination the ground underneath you that is supporting you right now.
- Is there any change? How is your body now?

- Repeat, 'I feel .... right now, I feel .... in my body. I am letting go of .... and I am grounding.'

Rock relaxation

Rock relaxation is a technique that can ground you quickly. It needs to be practised first and then used later as a relaxation trigger.

Sit in a chair or on the floor. Breathe deep breaths to relax you. Stay relaxed, yet alert and sit with your shoulders aligned with your hips and sit tall. Chin in and place your hands right over left on your solar plexus. This helps you to shift into a different perspective that can be helpful if you feel tired, bored, annoyed or stuck.

When you are imagining being somewhere it is important that you are looking out from your eyes and not looking at yourself. It is easier to connect with yourself and has a greater effect of calming you down.

Imagine sitting on a large chair-shaped rock, close your eyes, feel the rock supporting you, sense the support the rock is having on you internally and feel the quiet inside. Notice your breathing whilst on the rock and how good you feel. Keep practising this over again.

Whenever you remind yourself by sitting this way it will trigger your body memory of a relaxed and calm state.

Mindfulness and the body

Mindfulness is the non-judgemental nature of observing and is crucial to understand your internal experience and widening your window of tolerance without becoming overwhelmed.

It is easy to become entangled and sidetracked with emotions and sensations. Each time you slow down and pay attention to the body in the present moment the brain and body are being trained towards observation. This process inhibits emotional activation and is achieved by the prefrontal cortex down-regulating overwhelm, confusion or emotional triggers.

Do you prefer a beach or a wood or somewhere different? Think of that place in your mind – this is your happy place.

We are going to sit for 30 seconds and listen. Listen to any sounds in or outside the space you find yourself in. Is the air around you moving or is it still?

Imagine you are going for a peaceful walk (through your 'happy' place). You slow down your pace and take in the surroundings. Minding your step you are filled with the serenity and peace of the nature around you. As you walk, you go deeper into a calm place. See yourself walking slowly, take in the beauty and calm. As you walk, your mind slows down, your thoughts are slowing down and you are letting go of any busyness.

Notice your body sensations right now, feel yourself on the chair and feel how your body and weight make contact with the chair. Allow your breath to slow down. See if you can draw your attention into your body and be with the sensations right now. Allow anything busy or negative to melt away. Allow your awareness to travel outside you, allow the thoughts to melt and focus on the body sensations that are pleasant right now.

Start paying attention to your breath, notice that at the end of the in-breath there is a gap, a still point, where nothing happens at all. There you find yourself existing without thought. The same is happening at the end of the out-breath, there is a gap, a still point, where nothing happens at all. There you find yourself again existing without thought. Spend some time noticing the gaps.

Be present, feel what is truly going on; what is even better is that now you have a choice of what to be.

When you are ready, begin to bring your body back to the chair, the room and start to make tiny movements with the hands and feet.

Swallow or move your tongue around your mouth and open your eyes when you feel it is time.

Mindful walking

Getting out into nature has huge health benefits for our mental and physical well-being. So in addition to doing the previous exercise, try this whilst you are out in any green space.

Mindful walking is a walking meditation incorporating movement and mindfulness. Begin by standing still and tuning into your breathing, check in with how your body is feeling right now.

As you begin to slowly walk, bring your attention to your feet, from the heel to the toes. Feel them as you place them on the Earth. Move your awareness up to your body – slowly – and notice the sensations in your body as you are walking, even down to your fingertips. Control and slow your breathing.

Once you have connected with the sensations in your body, you can then begin to take your awareness out to your surroundings. If your mind wanders, bring it back to your breathing. See the beauty around you.

Ten minutes is all you need. Now, notice how you are feeling. What sensations are you aware of, do you feel calmer?

Severe trauma

If you feel unsafe in your body, or unable to connect with your own felt sense or have been diagnosed with a serious mental health issue then these exercises may not be enough. The first step is to seek professional help from practitioners who are 'trauma informed' and have experience in whatever you need help with. The exercises can be used alongside any other support you are receiving.

Some people struggle to even leave the house or be in large groups. If this is you, then your first step to recovery is the fact that you are reading this book. Your next step is to ask for help from someone you trust. Then you make it your mission to help yourself.

Feeling safe is a fundamental human need and it is impossible to function optimally if we do not feel safe. So begin with finding and connecting with a place you 'like' in either your own garden or corner of a favourite room in your house. This can become your safe place. Carry out the exercises in that space.

Moving the body is essential; mindful walking with your shoes off in your garden or anywhere in your house. Qi Gong, yoga or Taoist meditation are all good techniques to try and can all be found on YouTube; just follow the instructions on the videos. Try the exercises over several weeks and work out which ones suit you. We are all individuals and just because one person has said you should try it, doesn't mean it automatically works for you.

Self-help exercises are also readily available online and on the Tanfield Wellness website. Some of these exercises have been shared with me via Gail Donnan at The Wellness Gateway in Ripon, North Yorkshire for which I am extremely grateful.

Disclaimer
The information in this book is not a replacement for or a form of therapy, nor is it intended to cure, treat, or diagnose medical conditions. Meditation can, however, be a component of an overall treatment plan, when monitored by a healthcare professional.

The sacred site of Arbor Low in Derbyshire

7. VISITING SACRED SITES

The goal is not to be better than the other man, but your
previous self.
– Dalai Lama

Not only do we have energy within our physical bodies but there are organising forces, rhythms and flows. The Earth is made up of similar energy, elements and water. The Earth too is made up of 70% water. It also has lay lines, meridians and chakras!

Many people misinterpret their own energy when visiting sacred sites. Some even say the energy is not good. This is a brief word to help you to engage with your energy when visiting a sacred site.

I've been visiting the henges for a long time. In fact, I grew up living two fields away from the southern henge of the Thornborough Henges, in North Yorkshire, England. In my younger days, I didn't recognise the significance of the site. I certainly do now.

The Thornborough Henges are aligned using the same trajectory as Orion's Belt, so too are the pyramids of Giza. Other sacred sites around the world are also aligned with other constellations. I'm sure we only know a fraction about them but what is certain, because of the energy I feel there, is that they are incredibly important link with our Earth and the rest of our universe and beyond.

I have visited other sites in the UK, such as Arbor Low, Long Meg, Avebury and Glastonbury Tor, as well as the Thornborough Henges. At the busier sites, it feels like there's a lot of our human junk that's being dumped there. I sense the heaviness and the emotion. I douse to get the yes answer. It feels like we humans have been visiting these sites and offloading our woes, cleansing ourselves! So the first part of my visiting sites is often a clearing of this negative energy.

I also had three days over the spring Equinox in 2023 at Angkor Wat in Cambodia. 292 temples in a 100-square-mile radius. The energy there was incredibly strong. There are many sites all over the world and a significant sum in the UK. Please do make time to visit and connect in with them.

I'm going to explain what I do when visiting a site so it will help you connect in too, because in doing so, it naturally cleans you anyway! This is what I do; please do not feel that you have to copy. Go with your gut, feel with your senses and do what feels right to you.

When I set the intention that I am going to a sacred site I may feel a build-up of energy as the time gets closer. This is my soul getting excited, not my body telling me I shouldn't go (this happened recently when I went with a friend; she was misinterpreting the energy).

When I arrive, I may decide to sit in the car or stand nearby, allowing my system to settle with the energy there. I sometimes feel something in my body; I sit with it and let it settle.

I usually set sacred space (see page 136) then I check in with myself as to what is required. Quite often, I walk the perimeter either anticlockwise or clockwise, whatever feels right. It is important to do all of this in silence with a quiet mind. When I get a sense that I can go inside the sacred site, in my mind or out loud, I ask permission to enter it. Then I am just open as to what comes up, using my heart and soul and not my mind. I get a sense of whether something needs to be cleared or to connect to energy either within the Earth or in the cosmos.

Sometimes I may feel, hear or see. Sometimes, I see with my eyes open or sometimes with my eyes closed. I am open and keeping the ego mind at bay, I let information come in as to what is needed.

I walk slowly, mindfully and with respect, then I know where to be. Sometimes, I am on the edge, sometimes in the middle, and sometimes going inside is not what is needed.

I always connect in with my own heart, link down to the centre of the Earth, feeling my feet solid on the ground, then link in with the relevant constellation. And then I stay quiet and wait. I often feel a strong energy, either coming in through me or out. It feels like I'm connecting in with home. It can be emotional or you may be more aware of your body's sensations. All of this is you releasing as well as connecting. Sometimes, I see pictures and have an idea of what I connected to; other times I have to be satisfied with 'something happened'. Just go with your intuition and do everything slowly and mindfully.

Finally, I thank the energy of the site for the experience I have just had. It usually feels like I get a wave of appreciation back!

I USED TO BE NORMAL

8. RECOMMENDED READING LIST

There are many spiritual books for you to read, but I have highlighted a few and have split them into the ones to read when you are starting on your journey and others to read when you are further on your path. If anything feels like it is not true for you, pause it and then try it again later. It generally means you are not ready to receive the information. When you are ready, you will know it to be true. Also, bear in mind that what has been true for one person may not be anything to do with your path. Just listen with your heart and soul rather than your head.

Book suggestions for those starting their spiritual journey

- *Love Without Conditions* Paul Ferrini.
- *Falling Upwards* by Richard Rohr.
- *The Power of Now* by Eckhart Tolle – wonderful book about living in the present and not worrying about the past or future. Great for someone on the start of their spiritual journey.
- *Pathways to Wholeness* by Janet G Nestor.
- *Yeshua: One Hundred Meaningful Messages for Messengers* by Janet G Nestor – Jesus (Yeshua) spoke to Janet over 45 days in 2014. Janet is a physic intuitive based in North

Carolina and Yeshua channelled his messages and they will go straight to your heart. I read a few each night. Then I start back at the beginning.

- *The Emotion Code* by Dr Bradley Nelson – learn how to release trapped emotions within yourself, others and your animals. I used this form of dousing several times a day so I would consider this essential reading.
- *Many Lives, Many Masters* by Dr Brian Weiss.
- *I Wish my Doctor had told me this* by Kate Chator-Norris – empowering you to listen to your body and take health into your own hands.
- *The Monk Who Sold His Ferrari* by Robin Sharma – an easy read about money not being the 'be all and end all'.
- *Patriarchy Stress Disorder* by Valerie Rein – on the link between trauma, behaviour and emotions, with some useful exercises.
- *The Untethered Soul* by Michael Singer – on how we should be living our lives.
- *Reiki Healing for Beginners* by Karen Frazier.
- *The Four Agreements* by Don Miguel Ruiz.
- *Your Souls Plan* by Robert Schwartz.
- *The Re-Enlightenment* by Carole and David McEntee-Taylor.

And for those who are further along their spiritual journey

- *The Biology of Belief* by Bruce Lipton.
- *The Three Waves of the New Generation and the New Earth* by Delores Cannon – an absolute must.
- *The Individual and the Nature of Mass Events* by Jane Roberts (Seth). And other Seth Books – Jane Roberts channels Seth.
- *Hands of Light – A Guide to Healing through the Human Energy Field* by Barbara Ann Brennan.
- *Of Water and the Spirit* by Maliidoma Some.
- *Bringers of the Dawn* by Barbara Marciniak.
- *The Holiday From Hell* by Carole and David McEntee-Taylor.

Children's books

- *The Little Soul and the Sun* by Neale Donald Walsch.
- *Beautiful Girl* by Christiane Northrup.
- *The Protection: An invitation to Angels –* affirming angels to children and how they can help them feel safe.

Walk, talk, think, and act in love… always
– Yeshua: One hundred Meaningful Messages for Messengers
by Janet G Nestor

ACKNOWLEDGEMENTS

I am extremely grateful to all those who helped me with this book. To Carole McEntee-Taylor, a StoryTerrace writer, for her valuable help with the text and layout, and to all those clients who gave permission for their experiences to be told.

I'd also like to thank my friends, Linda and Malcolm, who proofread the final version.

To my husband who still says 'All I wanted was a normal wife', and to my children for their encouragement and support.

StoryTerrace

Printed in Great Britain
by Amazon